READY, SET, GO!

Published by CelebrityPress®, Orlando, FL.

CelebrityPress® is a registered trademark.

Printed in the United States of America.

ISBN: 978-0-9991714-0-0
LCCN: 2017947279

Most CelebrityPress® titles are available at special quantity discounts for bulk purchases for sales promotions, premiums, fundraising, and educational use. Special versions or book excerpts can also be created to fit specific needs.

For more information, please write:
CelebrityPress®
520 N. Orlando Ave, #2
Winter Park, FL 32789
or call 1.877.261.4930

Visit us online at: www.CelebrityPressPublishing.com

READY, SET, GO!

CelebrityPress®
Winter Park, Florida

CONTENTS

CHAPTER 1

PRACTICE THE MASTER SKILL

BY BRIAN TRACY

THE MASTER SKILL

Your ability to set and achieve goals is the Master Skill of success. A wise man said that "success is goals, and all else is commentary." A person with clear, written goals makes progress on even the roughest roads, but a person without goals makes no progress on the smoothest road.

UNLOCK YOUR POTENTIAL

This is a wonderful time to be alive. There are almost unlimited opportunities today for creative and determined people to achieve more of their goals than ever before. Regardless of short-term ups and downs in the economy and in your life, we are entering into an age of peace and prosperity superior to any previous era in human history.

Nature doesn't care about the size of your goals. If you set little goals, your automatic goal-achieving mechanism will enable you to achieve little goals. If you set large goals, this natural capability will enable you to achieve large goals. The size, scope, and detail of the goals you choose to think about most of the time are completely up to you.

TAKE CHARGE OF YOUR LIFE

The starting point of goal-setting is for you to realize that you have virtually unlimited potential to be, have, or do anything you really want in life if you simply want it badly enough, and are willing to work long enough and hard enough to achieve it.

The second part of goal-setting is for you to accept complete responsibility for your life, and for everything that happens to you, with no blaming and no excuses.

With these two concepts clearly in mind – that you have unlimited potential and that you are completely responsible – you are now ready to move to the next step, which is to design your future.

CLARIFY YOUR VALUES

One of the most important characteristics of leaders, and of the most successful people in every area of life, is that they know who they are, what they believe in, and what they stand for. Most people are confused about their goals, values and ideals, and as a result, they go back and forth and they accomplish very little.

Life is lived from the inside out. The very core of your personality is your values. Your values are what make you the person you are. Everything you do on the outside is dictated and determined by your values on the inside, whether clear or fuzzy. The greater the clarity you have regarding your values on the inside, the more precise and effective will be your actions on the outside.

What is most important to you in life? What are your values? What do you care about, believe in, and stand for?

ANALYZE YOUR BELIEFS

All improvement in your life comes from changing your beliefs about yourself and your possibilities. Personal growth comes from changing your beliefs about what you can do and about what is possible for you.

Self-limiting beliefs, sometimes based on a single experience or a casual remark, can hold you back for years. Most people have had the experience of mastering a skill in an area where they thought they had no ability, and being quite surprised at themselves. Perhaps this has happened to you. You suddenly realize that your limiting ideas about yourself in that area were not based on fact at all.

The most important belief for you to develop and hold onto is that you are a thoroughly good person, that you have unlimited potential, and that you are destined to be a big success in life. The more you believe these things to be true, the faster they will come true for you.

CREATE YOUR OWN FUTURE

Successful people look for the good in every situation. They know that it is always there. No matter how many reversals and setbacks they experience, they expect to get something good out of everything that happens to them. They believe that every setback is part of a great plan that is moving them inexorably toward achieving the great success that is inevitable for them.

If your beliefs are positive enough, you will seek the valuable lesson in every setback or difficulty. You will confidently believe that there are many lessons that you have to learn on the road to achieving and keeping your ultimate success. You'll therefore look upon every problem as a learning experience. Napoleon Hill wrote, "Within every difficulty or obstacle, there is the seed of an equal or greater advantage or benefit."

With this kind of an attitude, you benefit from everything that happens to you, positive or negative, as you move upward and onward toward achieving your goals.

What can you learn or gain from the biggest problems in your life today?

DETERMINE YOUR TRUE GOALS

The first step to goal achievement is for you to write it down. A goal that is not in writing is not a goal at all. Everyone who succeeds greatly works from clear, written, specific, detailed goals and plans, reviewed regularly. I personally recommend that you write and rewrite your goals each day, day after day, week after week, and month after month. This programs them deep into your subconscious mind where they take on a life and power of their own.

Continually ask yourself, "How will I measure success in the achievement of this goal? What standards will I set? What benchmarks or scorecards can I use to measure my progress?"

VISUALIZE YOUR GOALS CONTINUALLY

A key part of goal setting is for you to visualize your goal each day as if it were already attained. See your goal vividly in your mind's eye. Imagine what it would look like if you had already accomplished it. Get the feeling that you would have if you were at your goal already. Imagine the pride, satisfaction, and happiness you would experience if you were already the person you wanted to be, with the goal that you want to enjoy.

Repeat this visualization, combined with the feeling that goes with it, over and over during the day. Each time that you visualize and emotionalize, you program your goal deeper and deeper into your subconscious and superconscious minds. Eventually, your goal becomes a powerful unconscious force motivating and inspiring you day and night.

YOUR MAJOR DEFINITE PURPOSE

Your major definite purpose can be defined as the one goal that is most important to you at the moment. It is usually the one goal that will help you to achieve more of your other goals than anything else you can accomplish. It should have the following characteristics:

1) It must be something that you personally really want. Your desire for this goal must be so intense that the very idea of achieving your major definite purpose excites you and makes you happy.

2) It must be clear and specific. You must be able to define it in words. You must be able to write it down and know exactly what it is that you want and be able to determine whether or not you have achieved it.

3) It must be measurable and quantifiable. Rather than "I want to make a lot of money," it must be more like, "I will earn $100,000 per year by (a specific date)."

YOUR MOST VALUABLE ASSET

Your most valuable asset is your earning ability; your ability to apply your talents and skills in the market place. In reality, you could lose your home, your car, your bank account, and your furniture and be left with nothing but the clothes on your back. But as long as your earning ability was intact, you could walk across the street and begin generating a good living almost immediately.

Your earning ability is extremely valuable to you. And it can be either an appreciating asset or a depreciating asset. Your earning ability can grow in value if you continue to invest in it and develop it. It can decline in value if you begin to take it for granted and start to coast on the basis of what you have done in the past.

What one skill, if you developed and did it in an excellent fashion, would help you the most to double your income in the months ahead? Whatever it is, write it down and make a plan to develop that skill.

ACHIEVE YOUR FINANCIAL GOALS

One of your biggest responsibilities in life, something that you and only you are responsible for, is to manage your money, control your finances, and achieve financial independence in the course of your working lifetime.

This is not something that can be left to chance. The acquisition and deployment of money is governed by specific rules, principles, laws, and factors that are immutable and unchanging. Just is if you wanted to learn medicine, mechanics, or law, you would have to study the subject in detail for a long time in order to master it. You must give a lot of thought to money and finances or you will have shortfalls and problems in these areas all your life.

YOUR FAMILY AND RELATIONSHIP GOALS

The quality of your family life and your relationships will determine most of your happiness or unhappiness in life. Your goals in this vital area of your personal life cannot be left to chance.

Stand back and imagine that your family life and relationships were perfect in every way. What would they look like? How would your family life be different from what it is today? Imagine that you could wave a magic wand and create the perfect lifestyle with your family and relationships. What would it look like?

YOUR HEALTH AND WELLNESS GOALS

Your goal should be to enjoy high levels of health, fitness, and energy; to feel terrific about yourself, and to live a long, happy, pain-free life.

The starting point of achieving ideal levels of health and fitness is for you to make a decision to get into the best physical condition of your life, and then to maintain that level of physical conditioning and well-being indefinitely. Without this kind of firm decision, nothing happens. But if you make this kind of decision and stick to it, virtually everything is possible.

Clarity is essential. The greater clarity you have with regard to the person you want to be and the lifestyle you want to enjoy, the easier it is to make the necessary decisions and take the necessary actions to make those goals a reality.

MEASURE YOUR PROGRESS

It is absolutely amazing how much you can accomplish if you break your tasks down into bite-sized pieces, set deadlines, and then do one piece at a time, every single day.

In each area of your life, analyze your activities carefully and select a specific number that, more than anything else, determines your level of success in that area. Then focus all of your attention, all day long, on that specific number. The very act of focused attention will cause you to perform better in that area, both consciously and unconsciously.

Henry Ford said, "Any goal, no matter how large, can be achieved if you break it down into enough small steps."

BE PREPARED TO FAIL BEFORE YOU SUCCEED

Successful people fail far more often than unsuccessful people. Successful people try more things, fall down, pick themselves up, and try again – over and over again – before they finally win. Unsuccessful people try a few things, if they try at all, and very soon quit and go back to what they were doing before.

You should expect to fail and fall short many times before you achieve your goals. You should look upon failure and temporary defeat as a part of the price that you pay on your road to success, which you will inevitably achieve.

Identify all the obstacles that stand between you and your goal. Write down every single detail that you can think of that might be blocking you or slowing you down from moving ahead.

ASSOCIATE WITH THE RIGHT PEOPLE

Everything in life and business is relationships. Everything you accomplish or fail to accomplish will be bound up with other people in some way. Your ability to form the right relationships with the right people at every stage of your life and career will be the critical determinant of your success and achievement and will have an inordinate impact on how quickly you achieve your goals.

The more people you know, and who know you in a positive way, the more successful you will be at anything you attempt. One person, at the right time, in the right place, can open a door for you that can change your life and save you years of hard work.

Take every opportunity to network, to meet new people. Look for ways to help them achieve their goals. As Zig Ziglar said, "You can have everything you want in life if you just help enough other people get what they want."

MAKE A PLAN OF ACTION

Your ability to set goals and make plans for their accomplishment is the "master skill of success." No other skill will help you more in fulfilling your potential in achieving everything that you are able to accomplish.

All major accomplishments today are "multi-task jobs." They consist of a series of steps that must be taken in a particular order in order to accomplish a result of any significance. Even something as simple as preparing a dish in the kitchen with a recipe is a multi-task job. Your ability to master the skill of planning and completing multi task jobs will enable you to accomplish vastly more than most people, and is critical to your success.

Once you have determined you goal, make a list of everything you will have to do to achieve it, organize the tasks into a checklist, and begin working through your list, one step at a time.

MANAGE YOUR TIME WELL

To achieve all your goals, you must get your time under control. Time management is a skill set, and like any other, it is learnable. No matter how disorganized you have been in the past or how much you have tended to procrastinate or to get caught up in low-value activities, you can change.

You can become one of the most efficient, effective and productive people in your field by learning how others have gone from confusion to clarity and from frustration to focus. Through repetition and practice, you can become one of the most result-oriented people in your field.

The starting point of time management is for you to determine your goals and then to organize your goals by priority and value. You need to be absolutely clear, at any given moment, exactly what is most important to you at that time.

The second step is for you to set priorities on your activities, before you begin, and then to work non-stop until your most important task is complete.

REVIEW YOUR GOALS DAILY

Get a spiral notebook that you keep with you at all times. Each day, open up your notebook and write down a list of your ten to fifteen most important goals, without referring to your previous list. Do this every day, day after day.

The first day you write down your list of goals you will have to give them some thought and reflection.

Each day that you write down your list of ten to fifteen goals, your definitions will become clearer and sharper. You will eventually find yourself writing down the same words every day. Your order of priority will also change as your life changes around you. But after about thirty days, you will find yourself writing and rewriting the same goals every day.

Your subconscious and superconscious minds thrive on clear, written goals. Once you provide these goals, your unconscious minds go to work on them 24 hours a day, until they are accomplished.

UNLOCK YOUR MENTAL POWERS

Your ability to visualize is perhaps the most powerful faculty that you possess. All improvement in your life begins with an improvement in your mental pictures. You are where you are and what you are today largely because of the mental pictures that you hold in your conscious mind at the present time. As you change your mental pictures on the inside, your world on the outside will begin to change to correspond to those pictures.

You have been using the power of visualization continuously throughout your life. But the problem is that most people use visualization in a random and haphazard way, sometimes to help themselves and sometimes to hurt themselves.

Your goal should be to take complete control of the visualization process and be sure that your mind and mental images are focused continually on what you want to have and the person that you want to be.

PERSIST UNTIL YOU SUCCEED

Every great success in your life will represent a triumph of persistence. Your ability to decide what you want, to begin, and then to persist through all obstacles and difficulties until you achieve your goals is the critical determinant of your success. And the flip side of persistence is courage.

The history of the human race is the story of the triumph of persistence. Every great man or woman has had to endure tremendous trials and tribulations before reaching the heights of success and achievement. That endurance and perseverance is what made them great.

Successful businesspeople and entrepreneurs are all characterized by indomitable willpower and unshakable persistence.

SUMMARY

Decide today to realize your full potential in every area of life. Take a piece of paper and make a list of the goals you want to achieve in every area of your life. Select the one goal, your "Major Definite Purpose", that can have the most powerful positive impact on your life, and then do something every day that moves you toward that goal. This single exercise will change your life forever, and far faster that you can imagine.

About Brian

Brian Tracy is one of the top business experts and trainers in the world. He has taught more than 5,000,000 sales people in 80 countries.

He is the President of Brian Tracy International, committed to teaching ambitious individuals how to rapidly increase their sales and personal incomes.

CHAPTER 2

LIFE LESSONS FROM AN OUTBACK SHEARING SHED

BY ANDREW PHILLIPS

I learned my first lessons about goals, time management, and persistence in an Outback shearing shed. Growing up on an Australian sheep farm, our annual sheep shearing was a major event. With 2,500 acres, our family had thousands of sheep to be shorn every year. As the season came, we all worked tirelessly to bring the sheep from the distant paddocks closer to the shearing shed by driving them into yards and then into pens, in readiness to be fleeced by the shearers. When the itinerant workers arrived on our property, our kitchen hummed around the clock for the next several weeks with countless sandwiches, stews, cakes and pots of coffee.

I didn't know what to make of these unshaven, tough-looking men wearing blue singlets, double-thick, greasy jeans and shearer's boots. I watched them from the distance during 'smoko' – which was the shearers' break from work – for morning/afternoon tea and a smoke. Then, the summer I was 12, my father asked me if I wanted to work in the shearing shed. I liked the idea of having pocket money to go into town on Sunday to meet my friends, buy sweets at the general store and hopefully see the girl I had a crush on. I figured the job would help me achieve this. I didn't realize it at the time, but I had a goal!

THE ROUSTABOUT

Entering the shearing shed on my first day, I was hit with the combined smell of the sweaty shearers and the unwashed sheep's wool. The tin roof and the blazing sun made for stifling conditions. At 7:30 in the morning, the temperature was nearly 40 degrees Celsius and I had 10 hours to go!

The bell signalled the start of shearing and four men simultaneously raced into their designated pens, grabbing a sheep by the neck. While squeezing their legs around its body, they twisted it into a position to be dragged back out to their shearing station. Beginning with the sheep's belly, they would shear off the entire fleece in 2-3 minutes, then hurl the sheep down a slide into an outside pen. The fleece was shorn directly on to the wooden floor and I had only a few seconds to gather it up before the next sheep came into place. Picking up the heavy fleece correctly and casting it on to the wool table where it would be cleaned of burrs and mud is a learned skill which took me awhile to master.

The shed was a hive of activity with burly men swearing, clamouring after sheep and calling out, 'Where is the roustabout?' I was the roustabout and I scrambled quickly so I wouldn't get in their way. After collecting a fleece from the dirt-covered boards, I reversed direction to sweep the floor before the shearer pulled the next sheep from his pen. I was jostling like crazy to pick up the fleeces, one after another. I learned that the workers were paid per sheep and the best shearers would shear about 125 sheep a day. They worked fast and if I was in the way, they would shout at me, push me out of their section or knock me over flat. I had to move like lightening.

THE SHEARING SHED

I was the only roustabout for four shearers. I was inexperienced so I kept making mistakes and getting kicked and yelled at by these rough blokes. After the first day, I was completely exhausted and didn't think I was cut out to be a roustabout. I didn't want to show up the next day but I remembered my goal of going into town. I knew I needed a plan. I developed a system to improve by watching the patterns. I could move faster if I noted the rhythms of the shearers. It took me a week to get the hang of it and the shearers finally invited me to sit and eat with them.

Later I understood that they liked my ability to manage my time and persist. These farm workers were ultra-competitive and forever joking and teasing each other and me. They worked hard for a living, travelling around Australia, shearing sheep all year-round. The shearers were a team on a mission—nothing would stop them from earning their pay—especially a kid. I have always admired the shearers' work ethic and dedication.

A few weeks later, the shearers gave me a surprise initiation. Three of them suddenly grabbed me and one brandished the large ink blotter used on the wool bales to identify the farm and its wool. They thought it would be funny to paint me with the ink stamp. It wasn't pleasant but I knew then that they considered me a part of their team. I felt proud knowing that I had succeeded in my role as a roustabout. My planning and determination had paid off. I was enjoying the perk of seeing my mates in town with some coins in my pocket. I had reached my goal!

THE POWER OF GOALS

Despite the tough work, I began to look forward to this annual event. I developed skills as a roustabout and I felt good about contributing to my family's business. From my initial ambition of getting the pocket money to hang out with my buddies and buy treats, I moved on to wanting to earn enough to buy a new bicycle, then a motorcycle and later a business. Each year, I had a new aim which kept me motivated and every summer, I achieved my goals.

I didn't realize it at the time, but my successful outcomes were the result of striving for my objectives. Goal-setting became a habit for me. My experience showed me that the more I set goals and worked toward them, the more I could accomplish, and as I reached my targets, I felt more confident and optimistic. I later learned from Brian Tracy that personal goal-setting is the master skill of success.

I discovered that personal success is the result of two factors. The first is to determine exactly what you want. The second is to know the price you will have to pay to get it. Being clear about your goals is essential. Napoleon Hill says, 'There is one quality that one must possess to win, and that is definiteness of purpose, the knowledge of what one wants and a burning desire to achieve it.' I have found this to be true in my own life and it has been the case for those whom I have mentored. To achieve your goals, you must have clarity and a plan.

MANAGING TIME

As I learned in the shearing shed, if you do not have a plan for managing your time, you will not truly succeed at achieving your goals. If I hadn't mastered a system for collecting the fleeces and sweeping the floor efficiently before the next round of shearing took place, I would have slowed down the whole operation and certainly lost my job. Then I wouldn't have been able to hang out with my friends on the weekend. By predicting the consequences of doing or not doing something, I was able to determine the significance of focusing on a task and making it a priority.

An undertaking that is important to us has long-term consequences. It will help us achieve a future goal. A task which is not important does not have an impact on our future. We must learn to determine this key difference so that we concentrate daily on high-value activities. These actions will lead us toward reaching our clear goals.

As a 12-year old roustabout, I had to survive in sweltering, precarious conditions, endure ridicule and physical discomfort and persevere when I wanted to give up. I had to think quickly and prioritize my tasks. I continue to manage my responsibilities and take charge of my time by duplicating what I did when I worked in the shearing shed. When faced with challenges, I know that I can control my time by changing the way I think and work. I focus on the activities that really make a difference in my life.

Each day, I pay attention to my most important task at any moment and get started on it. I follow Mark Twain's idea that if the first thing you do each morning is to eat a live frog, then you can go through the day with the satisfaction of knowing that the worst part of your day is likely behind you. If we consider our 'frog' to be our most important task, then we know we must 'eat that frog' every morning. We can resolve to complete our most important objective and not procrastinate. This is a key strategy for not wasting time and we feel better knowing that we are using our time effectively. As Ben Franklin wrote, 'Do ye value life? Then waste not time, for that is the stuff out of which life is made.'

A ROAD MAP

As an entrepreneur and business coach, I have travelled around the world and many people have told me that they want to have a fulfilling career, raise children who are engaged citizens and have more free time to enjoy their leisure interests. They know that managing time, avoiding procrastination and setting goals are ways to accomplish these ambitions but they are not sure where to begin. I learned from Brian Tracy that the key to achievement is self-discipline and I have put this into practice in my own life.

By applying the principles of self-mastery as they relate to goals, planning and persistence, I consistently attain the targets that I set for myself. Of course, I have experienced setbacks along the way, but since I have a specific purpose, I keep going – whether it is to achieve a small goal of getting to the gym that day or a big goal of closing a sale.

I discipline myself to write out my goals every day and I schedule my time in advance. Writing out a plan is essential so you have a road map for where you want to go, just as the shearers went from property to property and aimed to shear a record number of sheep per day. I then prioritize my activities so that I am working on the most important task first. I know that managing my calendar allows me to get more done in less time and gives me free time to play tennis—my passion!

Since I was 20 years old, I have carried in my wallet this quote by Calvin Coolidge: 'Nothing in the world can take the place of Persistence. Talent will not; nothing is more common than unsuccessful men [and women] with talent. Genius will not; unrewarded genius is almost a proverb. Education will not; the world is full of educated derelicts. Persistence and Determination alone are omnipotent.'

I believe that persistence is absolutely the secret to success. As Brian Tracy says, 'persistence is self-discipline in action.' I learned this lesson in my first job as a roustabout and I have been persisting ever since! Having to manage my time in the fast-moving and aggressive environment of the shearing shed, taught me the importance of self-discipline and never giving up.

TAKE-AWAYS FROM THE SHEARING SHED

1. **Set Goals.**
   Define concrete timelines. Internalize why you want your goal. Break down the steps you need to take to accomplish it. Write out your goals every day. Make goal-setting a habit. Continually review your goals to make sure you are on track.

2. **Manage Your Time.**
   Make a timetable. Focus every day on the most important items you want to get done. Avoid procrastination. Every morning, accomplish your most important or difficult task for the day. Eat that frog!

3. **Persist.**
   Discipline yourself to work toward your goals every day. Overcome challenges. Keep a positive attitude. The rewards will be worth the short-term sacrifice. You will feel great when you have achieved each goal. You can do anything you set your mind to!

An optimistic, can-do outlook makes all the difference. Go forth with confidence and the discipline to reach your goals!

About Andrew

Andrew Phillips has specialized in sales training, franchising and professional development for 20 years. He is a highly-regarded international speaker, trainer and mentor in the fields of sales strategy, leadership, and business growth. Andrew works with organizations and individuals who are serious about achieving goals. His core values are old-fashioned hard work, gratitude, and integrity.

Based in Australia, Andrew oversees International Franchising for Brian Tracy Global and FocalPoint International Business Coaching. His role is to recruit, train and work with forward-thinking entrepreneurs throughout the world. The FocalPoint business coaching and corporate training programs offer complete excellence in professional education. Developed from 35 years of research by Brian Tracy, the system combines top-level professional development and business programs. These popular seminars in sales, leadership and professional coaching are proven to increase revenue and productivity. They are customized to client requirements and have over 5 million graduates worldwide. The most requested programs are *Perform at Your Best* and *Win Resales and Referrals*.

An experienced entrepreneur and a proponent of life-long learning, Andrew holds a Master of Management and a Master of Business Administration from the University of Adelaide. He leads by example and has logged over 10,000 training hours. Andrew's aim is to help other business owners achieve their goals of financial independence and make a lasting impact on their communities. A board member of the global Entrepreneurs' Organization, Andrew considers entrepreneurship to be the foundation of society.

Andrew resides in Adelaide with his wife and two daughters. He enjoys travel, reading, and especially tennis. Andrew can often be found courtside at the major tennis tournaments.

Contact Andrew at:
- aphillips@focalpointintl.com
- focalpointintl.com
- linkedin.com/in/andrewjphillips

CHAPTER 3

IMPOSSIBLE IS EASIER THAN YOU THINK

BY RAFAEL BADZIAG

I have to warn you. I am going to tell you some things about ultra running. I am using it only as an example. I absolutely don't want to talk anybody into it. If somebody feels inspired by it and comes up with crazy ideas, I am not taking any responsibility for it.

Do you know the difference between a marathon and an ultra marathon?

By definition, a marathon is a 42.2 kilometer run. Most people consider this distance as the maximum of human capabilities. And an ultra-marathon is everything above 42.2 kilometers: 50 kilometers, 80 kilometers and more.

Marathons are run on a flat street, while ultra marathons are run in difficult terrain, through mountains and deserts. You can physically prepare for a marathon and finish it without problems. But in an ultra-marathon, none of the participants can be sure he will finish. Even the best preparation can't protect you from suffering and unexpected crises.

The art of ultra running is the art of overcoming crises. It's the art of making your mind prevail over the weakness of your body. It's the art of suffering.

Three years ago, I learned I wouldn't make another year.

No, I wasn't sick. I am not going to tell you a doleful story. I simply decided to do something that by far exceeded my limits – to run an ultra marathon. An impossible undertaking, especially that I had been hardly running in the past at all, and I had been poor at sports at school.

I had no idea how to run 100km, especially in those conditions. How to do it? How to get down to it? I told my idea to my father. His reaction was immediate:

"100km? Running? In the desert? Are you crazy? Do you realize what kind of people go there? You are going to die there!"

Did you know that most people don't realize their dreams,
because they consider them as impossible to achieve?
And that's why they don't do anything to realize them.

Often, we think something is impossible because we simply don't know how to do it. I have a simple solution for that:

Ask somebody who has done it already!

I looked up in a phone book a two-time winner of the ultra race I wanted to run. I called him to invite him for coffee, so he could give me advice on how to train and what equipment to use. Though he didn't take me seriously at first, I didn't give up. After my third attempt, he finally relented. He not only explained everything to me, he even gave me some of his equipment.

After six months of cruel training and over a thousand kilometers run, we went to the 'African hell'. He won the race for the third time and I did something that I had considered impossible before: Despite the infernal heat and horrendous fatigue, I not only finished the race, but I placed in the top 30% of the field.

IMPOSSIBLE IS EASIER THAN YOU THINK

I realized that most of the limitations we are exposed to in our lives are not physical limitations imposed on us by the world or the laws of physics.

*Almost all limitations we are subject to
are mental limitations, limitations in our heads.*

If we think something is impossible, then, at first, it is just our thought, and the reality may be completely different.

"Impossible" is just an opinion.

Six months before, I considered running 100km to be impossible for me. I thought I would either collapse on the way, or give up and not make it to the finish line. In reality, it turned out to be absolutely doable of course … after the appropriate preparation.

I thought to myself: "I did something in sports that I had considered impossible before. Let's see then whether anything impossible can be done outside sports."

"HOW DO YOU START?"

100 years ago, at the beginning of the twentieth century, the wealthiest person in the world was Andrew Carnegie. Andrew believed that entrepreneurial success has its source in the mind and the personality of the entrepreneur himself. Fascinated by the young journalist Napoleon Hill, Andrew gave him a mission. He introduced Napoleon to the most successful entrepreneurs in America and asked him to construct the first philosophy of success, based on the interviews with these businessmen. Napoleon spent years talking to these richest people in the U.S.A., and after 20 years he published the results in his famous book, *Think and Grow Rich*.

Roughly 100 years later, I came up with the idea to do the same in the 21st century, i.e., to interview some of the best entrepreneurs, the wealthiest people, in order to find out the secrets of their success. But this time, I ventured to do it one level higher and to meet top businessmen not just from the United States but from all around the world. Here we are exclusively talking about self-made billionaires.

Great vision, but there is one hitch: Nobody has ever done anything like this before. Nobody has ever tried to. Why? Because the venture seems impossible to complete. Let's look at the stats:

Billionaires are an extremely rare breed. Statistically, only 1 in 5 million people in the world is a billionaire. A typical billionaire owns for example 200 hotels, 400 factories, 3,000 restaurants or 15,000 shops. The probability of meeting a billionaire by chance is comparable to winning the pot in a national lottery.

For the project, I needed to interview at least 20 billionaires. Do you know anybody who won the pot a in national lottery 20 times? Common sense tells us this is plainly impossible.

Can you imagine my anxiety and insecurity, when faced with this gigantic challenge? How to get to them? Where to start?

Then I got the first promising contact from a friend. It was a phone number belonging to a former employee of one of the billionaires. I needed to call him and convince him to put me in contact with the billionaire. I was procrastinating for weeks, gathering courage, weighing all pros and cons, putting off the call for later. I just couldn't overcome my fear. I was scared to make this first step, but…

FEAR IS THE WORST ENEMY OF SUCCESS

One of the tricks I use in my various challenges is the so-called "promise card." I wrote on the card my promise: "I will write and publish a world bestseller by the end of June 2016." And I put my signature on the back. I printed two dozen of these cards, laminated them and distributed them among friends, so that they could keep me accountable for that promise. I always carry one with me so I don't forget about my main challenge.

I made these cards when procrastinating with the call, and I gave one of them to the friend who gave me the phone number. His reaction changed my life beyond recognition. He said: "Listen! I gave you a contact to a billionaire. And you are giving me some damn scrap of paper instead of calling and taking action? Come on, pull yourself together! Get serious!"

And I humbly took the phone and called the guy.

And this way, my great adventure started. Since then, astonishing things happened. I have travelled several times around the world and I regularly meet its wealthiest inhabitants. Today, I personally know and have met

25 billionaires. Do you know anybody who won the pot in the national lottery 25 times? The richest people on the planet spend time with me, invite me to their homes for lunch or dinner, send me Christmas cards or call me.

If somebody told me four years ago what my life would look like today, I would declare him insane. And all that happened because of what this friend made me realize:

The gap between ignorance and knowledge is much less than the gap between knowledge and action.

IT'S NOT ABOUT KNOWING, IT'S ABOUT DOING!

So:

1. Take action now, just do it!
2. Overcome your fear and make the first step – even if you don't know the next step!
3. Take a risk even without any guarantee of success!

What else can we learn from this story?

That…

Independently of how improbable a goal is,
your directed action can bend the probability in your favor.
And what seemed impossible becomes possible for you.
~ Rafael Badziag

IMPOSSIBLE IS EASIER THAN YOU THINK

I often ask billionaires what achievement they are most proud of in their lives.

For me, the achievement I am most proud of is finishing a 111-kilometer non-stop run through the Sahara Desert in 105° Fahrenheit (40°C) heat. It is called the Sahara Ultra 111. At the same time, it was the most traumatic experience in my life. Never in my life, have I suffered as much as during this run.

But apparently, I was not alone. It was a borderline experience not just for me. The field consisted of the best European ultra-runners ... except for me, an amateur. Despite that, almost half of the participants gave up due to circulatory collapse, dehydration or sunstroke. The majority of those who finished had lost their consciousness along the way.

Before the start, these pros were looking at me wondering what I was doing there. They were aware of what was ahead of us and thought there was no chance I would finish that race. And indeed, the run turned out to be an ordeal as I started with an injured knee. After only 20 kilometers, I already had wounds on my soles and blood was squelching in my shoes.

At kilometer 32, I realized it was over. I was prepared for a crisis after 60 kilometers, but at 32? I sank into despair. How was I going to run another 80 kilometers, if after 32 kilometers I was already at the end of my rope. I was getting stuck in the sand. I couldn't breathe due to a jammed nerve. I was limping. With every step, pain in my knee paralyzed me, and my feet went numb. And on top of it, I was boiling in my own sweat.

I decided to quit.

But then, I realized that I had told all my friends about the race. Remember the "Promise card"? And now they were crossing fingers and cheering for me. After finishing several ultra marathons, I had a reputation for being a tough guy. And now, should I give up? What am I going to tell them? I had a knee pain? It was simply not an option!

I consciously opted for another 16 hours of torture without any guarantee of finishing the race. I decided to push on as long as I was still conscious – while on the verge of collapsing.

If you want to do the impossible, cut off your way back
and put yourself in a situation of no return.

And now, the worst, the hottest part started. It was in 105° Fahrenheit (40°C) in the shade ... but there was no shade. I was literally reeling, exhausted and overheated. I was in agony, had hallucinations. I realized now, it's really over.

And then I recalled Winston Churchill's words:
"If you are going through hell, keep going!"

And these words saved me. I realized that in ultra runs as well as in life:

*Success is achieved by those who don't give up
and fight until they achieve it.*

So, I repeated to myself Churchill's motto over and over again:

"Never, never, never give up!"

And now my goal was just to take another step and another, and another ... and not drop from exhaustion ... and try not to think of how many steps there are ahead. Of course, on the way to the finish line, I experienced several other crises. Despite that, I managed to reach the finish line at kilometer 111. It took me 21.5 hours of hellish struggle. During the run, I drank over 5 gallons (20 liters) of water and lost 12 pounds of my body weight.

As of today, only three people in the world have managed to finish this ultra run without fainting. I am proud to be one of them.

I realized that…

*Even when you think it's over and there is no way you can
continue, when you are at the end of your rope and can't take
any more pain, it doesn't really mean it's over. In reality,
you can endure much, much more.*

In my case, I thought it was already over at kilometer 32. In reality, I could run 80 kilometers more, up to the finish line at kilometer 111.

WE CAN DO MUCH MORE THAN WE REALIZE

I realized how far in our everyday lives we are from the limits of our capabilities, how little from our enormous potential we usually exploit. If we can only force ourselves to come close to our limits, we are able to astonish the world and ourselves.

Because. . .

"Only those who will risk going too far can
possibly find out how far one can go."
~ T.S. Eliot

Which of your dreams do you consider so improbable that you are afraid to go for it – for fear of failure? When will you dare to take the first step? After death? Or maybe, you would prefer to experience this magic as long as you are alive? The magic to do the impossible, to achieve even the most improbable of dreams.

We can act only in the present. It's in the here
and now that we can create the future and make our dreams
of today become the reality of tomorrow.
~ Rafael Badziag

But tomorrow may never come. So, don't put it off. Make the first step today!

And remember:

IMPOSSIBLE IS EASIER THAN YOU THINK !

About Rafael

Rafael Badziag is a Germany-based global entrepreneur, motivational writer, speaker and angel investor. In the late nineties, he built his first multi-million-dollar business Raddiscount.de pioneering e-commerce in Europe. It was the first bike online-shop in Germany, which he developed into an established business in the German speaking market. He then expanded his ventures into an array of internet-based services and products in several countries.

His passion is learning his limits and crossing them, as well as learning the limitations of the people around him and helping them to overcome those.

Rafael is founder of the NoLimits project, where he fights against the limitations of his body, mind and soul. You may find him sprinting on a treacherous mountain trail, running a 111 km ultra-race across the Sahara Desert, or dancing a tango on the floor of a fancy Milonga. On his English blog, NoLimits.co, he describes his extreme experiences and inspires others to follow his example, to also undertake challenges and to reach seemingly unachievable goals. The motto of this project is given by T.S. Eliot's words: "Only those who will risk going too far can possibly find out how far one can go." The mission here is to inspire readers to live their lives fully with passion and zeal, to make them leave their limits behind, so they can rise above the boundaries of mediocrity and experience their full potential, exceptional success and deep satisfaction in their lives.

His expeditions and remarkable journeys have taken him several times around the world, from the ice desert of Antarctica through the hottest deserts on the planet to the Peaks of the Seven Summits. He has visited over 50 countries and all seven continents.

Rafael has given the second-most popular TED Talk in the history of his country with over 1 million views.

Recently, Rafael has been travelling the world and meeting the world's most successful entrepreneurs, all of them self-made billionaires, from various regions, industries, cultures, religions and age groups. He managed to open the most inaccessible doors and got access to some of the wealthiest people on the planet. By conducting face-to-face interviews with them, he was able to obtain first-hand information on their methods and mindsets. He reveals their success secrets on his website, TheBillionDollarSecret.com, the corresponding YouTube channel as well as the upcoming book with the same title.

Some people call him, *The Napoleon Hill of the 21st Century*, others – *The Billionaire Magnet.* His writing and business activities have a truly global scope.

Rafael is a member of the National Association of Experts, Writers & Speakers.

In order to learn more about Rafael's recent activities, visit his English websites:
- http://TheBillionDollarSecret.com
- http://NoLimits.co

Or watch his YouTube channel:
- http://youtube.com/TheBillionDollarSecret

You can contact Rafael at:
- Tel: +49 175 569 5615
- Email: rafael@nolimits.co
- LinkedIn: https://linkedin.com/in/rafaelbadziag

CHAPTER 4

TEN BUSINESS SUCCESS SECRETS FOR CREATIVES

BY TRACY AND SONYA SAYWELL

People who are creative have a lot to offer the world of business but they might not know it. Some of our most talented designers and artists fail because they have "no business sense." Yet the creative process they know so well contains many elements essential for success.

During the years of running our own businesses, helping hundreds of students through both creative and business challenges, we have learnt that the same skills that make you thrive as a creative can help you thrive in business – if only you know how to apply them. Come with us for a sneak peek into our creative world to see what business secrets can be learnt. . .

Success Secret #1:
JUST GET STARTED!

My daughter, Sonya, and I design resort wear and decorator items and run a college for creatives. My day starts early in the morning while Sonya works late into the night. At dawn, you'll find me in my studio mixing bright watercolours and inks, pouring them on paper and watching the colours explode into each other – bougainvillea pinks and ocean turquoises, shadowy purples and cool greens. It's the chemistry of my own excitement and the materials themselves that motivates me. When you are creative and you love your art, you never have a problem getting

43

started. Your passion drives you. Your ideas light up the world in front of you and you just start moving forwards. This creative excitement is exactly what's needed for business. A spirit of adventure and play where you don't have to know everything before you start.

Success Secret #2:
MISTAKES ARE MARVELLOUS

Approach your business with the same sense of exploration and excitement you do all your creative projects.

Unpredictability is a magical part of the creative process, especially when you work with inks and watercolours. We're never quite sure which way the water will run or how the pigments will disperse. It's spontaneous and playful - new possibilities emerge right in front of our eyes. Not everything is under control, and that's what makes it so fascinating. We make mistakes but we're not concerned. Mistakes open up new ideas, new directions. Business can also be this unpredictable. Things don't always flow the way you were thinking but that doesn't have to be a bad thing.

Just like in your studio, in your business you can discover treasure hidden in the mistakes you make. The journey is meant to be surprising.

Success Secret #3:
YOU ARE YOUR BRAND

Sonya and I live in Australia on the Gold Coast. It's a subtropical environment with the longest golden beach you could ever see, hundreds of waterways and canals and amazing bird life. Holiday makers come here all year round for the water sports, to unwind, and relax by the pool. It's our own backyard but we never take it for granted. We travel a lot and each time we return home we see it with fresh eyes. It's part of us.

The resort wear and decorator items we design are inspired by the colour and energy of this place. Our water colours are the basis for our range of colourful textile designs and prints – silk chiffon dresses that flow in the breeze; active wear; bright cushions and happy furnishings that celebrate the beauty of our local experience. It's what makes our work unique. Everyone is looking for what makes their work unique in business as well. They want to stand out in the market place. When you are creative, you come with uniqueness built in. You infuse your values and personality into everything you do. You are your point of difference.

It's where you live and breathe, what you do and how you do it. Every moment is your creative business.

Success Secret #4:
YOU CAN'T DO IT ALL

Of course, getting from an ink splash to a final product such as a designer evening dress is not always easy. It requires the help of many others to bring ideas into reality. The designs have to be scanned and sent to manufacturing companies for proofing and printing. Adjustments must be made for different types of materials. Product patterns have to be created, finalised and sampled, photo shoots organised, websites designed, products advertised, orders fulfilled, accounts paid and problems solved. It's impossible to do all these jobs ourselves so we delegate and outsource. We focus our creativity on making the decisions that count and we don't weigh ourselves down with jobs that are best given to someone else. We see it all as our creative process, only now our artistic materials have expanded to include a range of talented people who are specialists in their own fields.

Even the most solitary of creatives knows that eventually the time comes when their work has to be handed over to others in order to be borne into the world. Creative success means picking the moment to do this and making the business experience a streamlined extension of your process.

Success Secret #5:
RENEW YOUR VISION

In recent years, our design experiments have diversified while at the same time, our underlying purpose has crystallised. It's true to say the essence of our purpose has always been there, just not always put into words. There is a moment, however, when it feels right to articulate your mission more clearly. The first time we did this, we were away from home and that gave us a fresh perspective, like standing back from a painting so you can see the whole instead of just the detail. We could see clearly that our work was about being creative ambassadors for where we live and being inspiring mentors to other creatives. Now it's an annual event to let go of our current activities for a while and regroup around what's important. To make business an ongoing success, these moments of vision and renewal are essential.

Make a regular time for an 'artistic critique' of your activities as a whole. Check that you are creating your best life, then set your goals for the future with confidence and commitment.

Success Secret #6:
MAKE TIME FOR COMPLETIONS

Like many other creatives, Sonya and I get excited about too many projects at once. It's nothing to visit our studio and find an underwater scene on the watercolour desk, parrot feathers on the sketch board and half-finished fashion figures in the big canvas studio. On our schedule might be a silk scarf production run; an art kit and course; a floor rug project; a gym wear experiment; and preparation for an exhibition. Day and night, everything we see sparks a new creative direction. It's so engaging, yet if we followed every new idea, there would be no time for completion.

Learn to love your completions as much as your ideas. Remember that the completion phase moves a lot more slowly than the crazy-fast idea phase. There'll be contingency plans, painstaking adjustments, problem solving and unexpected outcomes. You'll need patience to work through it all. You'll need flexibility as well. Your ideas may have to be adapted to the material world much more than you initially thought. This is where your purpose and goals can help you focus and stay on track. However, goals are only one part of the solution. Following your work through to completion requires another important element: self-belief.

Success Secret #7:
BELIEVE IN YOURSELF

One of the core reasons so many promising artists abandon their dreams is lack of self-belief. They never stop having ideas, but they never quite complete them either. By staying in the idea phase and chopping and changing projects all the time they can avoid completion and the exposure to failure they most fear. To move past this, it's important to find a much greater resolve. You need something that will see you through all the challenges that come with making an idea real.

. . . but as a creative, think about this. Don't just believe in yourself as a successful 'artist' or 'business person.' What's more important is to believe in your ability to learn and grow. Failing is an inevitable part of every material endeavour. You can fail as an artist and you can fail as a business person but you can't fail as someone who is willing to learn and grow. You can only thrive from whatever happens. Take a moment to let that sink in.

Success Secret #8:
PROFIT IS CREATIVE

So, let's recap here. If you're a creative and you've applied the secrets so far, you've tapped into your sense of adventure and made a start. You've discovered new ideas hidden in your mistakes. You've recognised your innate uniqueness and 'owned' that as your brand. You've found people to help you and made them part of your creative process. You've crystallised your purpose, practiced following through and you have an unshakeable belief in your ability to learn and grow. It's not a big stretch now to see that you can profit from your work.

Money is one of the many exciting variables you have to play with in your creative business. It's not at the opposite end of the spectrum of creativity. It's an integral part of the creative process. If you are not making as much money as you would like, then it's time to explore your profit variables just as though they were colours on your palette. With the same creative approach you know so well, you can try new things, talk to new people and be inspired by the examples of other artists and mentors. The profit margin is the place where you find the win/win/win for you, your audience and your wider environment and there's so many fun ways to work in this space.

Success Secret #9:
PREPARE TO PIVOT

Unlike the chopping and changing we talked about earlier, the ability to change when you need to - even pivot 180 degrees to face a whole new direction - is a business essential. In business, everything changes. Government regulations, industry trends, technology, competitors, the economy and buyer behaviour are forever in motion. You can't afford to get stuck on one idea. If something isn't working, you must pivot. What you need to know is that pivoting requires an anchor to move around. In your life, that anchor is your purpose. It's your creative core. When you understand your core, everything else can be open to change yet you will still get to where you are going.

Success Secret #10:
BUSINESS IS YOUR PASSION!

So, now you have had a glimpse into our creative world and the insights we've gained both from our businesses and from observing hundreds of wonderful creatives that have passed through our doors. We hope you've seen how creativity is an essential ingredient for business success, not just in product design but in every aspect of business. If you are now excited about the possibilities of standing out in the crowd by taking a creative approach to everything in your business from your customer experience to your systems and processes; your marketing strategies and all the nitty gritty things; even the 'boring' stuff, then congratulations! You've discovered Success Secret Ten for creatives – business is your passion!

. . . And you can be great at it.

HERE IS A SUMMARY OF OUR 10 SUCCESS SECRETS:

Secret 1 - Just Get Started.

Secret 2 - Mistakes Are Marvellous.

Secret 3 - You are Your Brand.

Secret 4 - You Can't Do It All.

Secret 5 - Renew Your Vision.

Secret 6 - Take Time for Completion.

Secret 7 - Believe in Yourself.

Secret 8 - Profit is Creative.

Secret 9 - Prepare to Pivot.

Secret 10 - Business is Your Passion!

About Tracy and Sonya

Tracy and Sonya are a mother and daughter team of fashion business creatives. Tracy began her career in the fashion business with her mother, Peggy. Now Sonya is carrying on the tradition with Tracy. Of course, the scope of their creativity has evolved greatly over four decades in the industry. What started out as a small chain of exclusive fashion boutiques in country Australia, led to experiments in fabric design, a fashion label, and a well-known college for creatives with campuses on the Gold Coast and in Brisbane, Australia. In 2005, Tracy and Sonya entered the Australian Fashion Design Awards with their own label. They stood out as finalists in three categories - Fashion on the Field; Designer Collections and Couture and won the coveted Rising Star Award. Their entry was a perfect example of what they love most. Bright, free-flowing silk chiffon fabrics, hand painted with their own colourful designs and sewn into elegant, relaxed dresses ideal for warm summer evenings.

Since that success, they have continued to celebrate the colour and life of their local area through their art work; surface designs and clothing labels while at the same time mentoring many other young creatives to win awards and build successful careers of their own. Fostering creatives into successful businesses is as much a passion for Tracy and Sonya as their own creative adventures. Their students have gone on to accomplish success in all aspects of the design industry from shoe design, to handbag innovation, bridal wear and textile designs for high-quality outdoor fabrics that are now being picked up by international hotel chains and boating companies.

Tracy's excitement at empowering others began right at the beginning of her career. She saw that creating a great experience for customers was what made business most rewarding. Although she started with very little, she saw that she could make the customer experience better, make it more exciting and more creative, always giving 150% to everyone that came in her door. That same enthusiasm and generosity transfers to her work as a business and creative mentor.

Growing up in this passionate and creative environment, Sonya was a natural at creating gorgeous colour schemes and eye-catching patterns, but her secret passion was in what she calls "the ultimate way to be creative" – the design of a whole business not just the product. Sonya gets as much excitement out of innovating business systems; improving the experience of people and transforming the whole life cycle of a product as she does from paint-and-paper moments in her studio.

Together, Tracy and Sonya know that creatives really want to learn about business from other creatives. Their next adventures involve a more global out-reach through online courses and activities, where mentoring in entrepreneurship can make a positive difference not only to creatives and their businesses, but to a wider system of communities across the world.

You can connect with Tracy & Sonya at:

Australian Institute of Creative Design
- www.aicd.edu.au

Fashion Label Success
- www.fashionlabelsuccess.com

Paint Art That Sells
- www.howtopaintartthatsells.com

Tracy Saywell
- www.tracysaywell.com

CHAPTER 5

MY LUCKY POWER OF THE MIND

BY TATYANA ZBIROVSKAYA

Whatever the mind of man can conceive and believe, it can achieve.
~ Napoleon Hill

Some say I'm lucky, but I know the only luck I've had is realizing the power of my mind. Ever since I was a little girl reading fairy tales, I believed in miracles. Fear never even crossed my mind! I always strived for best thoughts, desires, and actions. It is this that has led me to the greatest people and events. It has always helped sculpt my life, guiding me from my small hometown in Siberia, snuggled up against the Altai Mountains, and into a magnificent life journey of self-discovery and seeking that which I viewed in my mind.

Today, people often enquire about how I've managed it all—the wonderful and the challenging. It seems almost impossible to the logical, processed mind to go from a relatively isolated area in the world where opportunity was given selectively to a country where I am today.

It began with living by the Law of Attraction, even before I fully understood what it was or how it worked.

THE POWER OF ATTRACTION

We're all energy in this world, and the way we choose to think and process what happens to us is how we create the experience we have.

To some, the Law of Attraction is spiritual nonsense. If this is your thought, I cannot change that. However, I take delight and optimism in extending you the challenge to think "what if". It may change your life in a way you once thought was left for others, not you. In my life, it helped me in achieving that I once only envisioned, but always believed would happen.

I was born and raised in a remote Siberian town in the middle of the Cold War and a Communist Regime. I lived with my grandmother in a wooden house, without inside plumbing or television. She was a tailor and had only four years of education. We used a brick stove for cooking and heating, and shared the outhouse and the water pump with two other families. My parents split before I was born. My grandmother raised me because my mother served as a Navy Doctor on a vessel that traveled the world. I didn't even meet her until I was six!

Everyone I knew was poor. Post-war Russia was a tough environment for most. I recall standing in the freezing cold winter for hours just to buy a small piece of bread. The only news was from Soviet newspapers such as *Pravda*. Like most, we'd lost family members to the political system and the war, and it created great hardship for everyone.

I had no siblings and no children of my age to play with. Older kids were often cruel to me; they weren't evil, merely having a hard time … we all were. I instinctively understood them without judgment and empathized with everyone, regardless of their "faults". I craved their acceptance. In return, people loved me back. My mindset of a happy child gave me the gift of a happy childhood.

I realized this ability to survive these tough times and process things differently came to me when I was focusing on what I want, and it felt good; everything would work out by itself, even if I didn't know it was called the Law of Attraction.

MAKING THE MOST OF OUR MOMENTS

Why certain things come into our lives the way they do?

When you breathe in and think about the moments of your life that make it up as a whole, do you see just those powerful, big, defining moments that shaped your journey? Or, do you see a combination of big, defining moments mixed with the little ones that really give you a complete picture?

Being open to how small occurrences help us grow allows us to expose ourselves to meaningful experiences. You cannot be so busy while looking for the mountain that you miss the diamond by your feet.

As a kid, I loved dancing and gymnastics, but I could never do the full split. One night, I suddenly felt overwhelming knowledge that I could do it. I got out from under the warm blanket onto the freezing floor and did the splits, just like I'd always been able to. By morning, I couldn't. My mind was no longer set the right way. I doubted myself, and I failed, but I remembered the feeling of power.

Another time, at age eleven in the first days of our short Siberian summer, I went to the beach along the river with two friends. The river still carried chunks of ice in it that flowed down from the Altai mountains. Most brave beachgoers only went in the water up to their waist, just long enough to urinate and retreat back to their towels. Not me, I wanted to see the other side. Suddenly, I absolutely knew I could swim across. And... I did! However, I didn't take into account the troubles along the way, such as a strong current and a huge barge just about sucking me under. It was during this event that I realized that once in a while there is a difference between knowing you can do something and actually do it. Even if the barge hadn't come along, that current was very challenging. But I did it!

Now, as I've grown wiser I spend more time understanding the nuances of the Law of Attraction, Quantum Physics, etc. I wanted to learn how to use this to create my future. Drawing from the experiences of my splits and the river, I recalled one thing they had in common—the feeling of power and knowledge I had.

I started to experiment on how I could intentionally attract the experience using the power of the mind. Here is one of many examples. I was overcome with the desire to ride a horse. There is something about being on the back of a beautiful horse, my face to the sun and feeling that freedom that comes with riding one that drew me in. I craved it.

I took only a minute to indulge in the thought of it, visually placing myself on that horse, petting its neck, feeling the sensations of riding it—the wind in my hair, the contentment in my heart, and the liberation of the experience—just like in movies. And I forgot about it.

The next day I was at the park where no horses were allowed. Suddenly, through the bushes, a rider in his hat on a horse appeared. It was like a fairytale. He stopped in front of me. "You can pet the horse," he said. I was stunned. A few moments later, the horse, crossing a small bridge, unexpectedly stopped, and... deposited her droppings right in the middle of that small bridge. The man got off to clean it up.

I said, "Just yesterday I was dreaming about riding a horse."

"Did you?" he asked. "Well, hop on up." Next minute I was riding the horse. Miracle?

But what about those big, defining moments?

I've always had a great passion to be a performer. Since kindergarten, I enjoyed reading and telling stories to kids, watching their jaws drop in amazement, and dreamt of becoming an actress. After finishing high school at sixteen years old, I defied my grandmother's wishes, took a plane to Moscow and applied to Russia's best acting academy. Without any friends or connections in the huge, strange city, I was a face in the crowd of thousands of applicants from across the Soviet Union. But my mind knew I had the power to succeed, and I'd learned not to doubt it. After months of competition, I became one of twenty finalists!

Now I lived in Moscow, the nation's cultural center, learning the fine art of acting from the best professors our theatrical tradition had to offer. I was performing daily on the best stages in front of thousands and rubbed shoulders and became friends with outstanding creative talents. I even once performed in the Kremlin. It was a fairy-tale life that started with the power of my mind.

MY PURPOSE REVEALED

When one lives life fully, they cannot help but wish to pass that gift on to others.

A time came when I wanted to bring a baby into the world—a boy or girl didn't matter—but they would be the best and brightest, a miracle. I married a man that was smart, intelligent, and desirable in many ways. With him, I could have a child that would have all these strengths and creative genes in it.

It was then I learnt that some things cannot be controlled. My beautiful baby boy was born with a rare genetic disease. There was no cure; the doctors predicted four years of life for him in constant physical pain, followed by death.

I felt the earth burst into fire under my feet. I spent the following year living with my baby in various hospitals, as he was undergoing multiple life-threatening surgeries. In those corridors, I was just another anguished face in the crowd, among many other grief-stricken mothers. The pain and suffering in those halls was immense.

There were wonderful doctors in Russia, but no medicine or equipment to help my boy. Abandoning my acting career and moving where I could get help was a small price to pay for even a chance to save my boy. Miracles began to happen, and a year later I was settling in New Jersey, with nothing to my name and only some rudimentary English. I took odd jobs and cared for the elderly to support my family. It was hard, but I loved being in America. I felt so much compassion and love from everyone. So many Americans helped and welcomed us with open hearts. Of course, my son always attracted good vibrations everywhere we went. He was a funny and happy kid, sending kisses to everybody who asked, and even to those who didn't.

American healthcare was able to add five precious years to my son's life. Instead of only four years, he lived nine happy years – all of which I treasure. While I'd tried to prepare for his death, it hit me really hard. I was devastated. My life felt over. I'd also gotten divorced. I was alone. I thought I had nothing to live for anymore.

It took me time to get back on track, when I finally knew it was time to take action again. I went back to school, immersed myself in computer science and learned programming languages. My mind was set on becoming an independent professional, and I ended up having great jobs at several prestigious US companies, but eventually settling at NYU Medical Center to build databases for neuroscience research. I worked there with some of the most inspired and brightest scientists in the world. Another dream came true. That's where I've learned a lot about our brain.

Now that I lived in New York City, it reminded me of my dream of acting, which never faded. I had to pursue it. I worked during the day and rehearsed at night, but roles for Russian-speaking actors were few. I needed a different approach, so I began writing for myself and entered the stand-up comedy circle. Soon I became a finalist in a Tristate Stand-Up Comedy Competition. This exposure led to some small roles, mostly in television and movies, and often alongside American greats.

After taking filmmaking courses at NYU, I also wrote, directed, and produced a short feature that was accepted into the "Short Film Corner" at the Cannes Film Festival. Finally, I was offered a speaking role at New York Metropolitan Opera. I resigned from my programming job, which I've learned to love, but it was time to move on. And NBC flew me to Chicago for a part in their popular TV series, *Chicago Fire*.

Still, I felt there was more for me, and my heart began opening up to new opportunities. I was invited to teach drama and creativity at the prestigious Pushkin Academy in New York City. Being among these energetic and joyful children, who expressed their thoughts and feelings without reservation or judgment, was as educational and inspiring for me as my drama lessons were for them.

WE ARE THE PRODUCT OF OUR THOUGHTS

We are what we think. All that we are arises with our thoughts.
With our thoughts we make the world.
~ Buddha

Heartache and tough lessons are a part of life. Everyday, I know a little bit more about the power of the mind and using it to achieve success and attract opportunities. Embracing the lessons and experiences that rise up through the ashes of despair—much like a Phoenix is reborn—make the difference. People have more inner power than they realize; they just don't know how to open it up. You can start your life over at any time you desire, regardless of your age or circumstances.

When one lives life fully, one cannot help but pass that gift on to others. My son's life, though short, revealed to me the purpose of my own life. He gave me infinite amounts of love and joy the best way he could, and passed it on to others too. He taught me unconditional love. That was his life's purpose and now it is my purpose to carry on.

Children are usually born with all the right mind powers; they are natural dreamers. They instinctively live like little superheroes until adults step in and suppress that. This can be reversed if adults relearn their powers from children. Some teach these principles through academic books. There is a lot of research done and many good books written on neuroscience, quantum physics, Law of Attraction, Power of the Mind, etc. I've learned a lot from these books, my studies and my personal experience. I would like to share my knowledge through visual examples, as well as life stories, activities, and dance.

We are defined by our thoughts. If you want your life to be a masterpiece, think of your thoughts as the strokes on its canvas. If you don't like what you paint, you always can start your masterpiece again with a clean canvass.

What we think – matters! We're like a radio station. Positive signals generate a positive feedback, while broadcasting misery attracts even more misery.

The Russian playwright Anton Chekhov penned: "Don't tell me the moon is shining; show me the glint of light on broken glass." In English, this concept is known as, "Show, don't tell!" This inspires my latest project, a production company that makes educational, animated videos introducing children to the Power of their mind and how to utilize the Law of Attraction in a clever, fun way. If children would retain this power and teach adults about it, imagine what our world could become . . .

About Tatyana

Tatyana Zbirovskaya was born in the remote Siberian town of Biysk. The child of a poor, broken family, she was brought up by her grandmother. She loved fairy tales and believed early on that she could accomplish anything she set her mind on. At eleven years old, on a whim, she made local news by swimming across the wide, ice-cold river. After finishing high school at sixteen years old, she took a plane to Moscow and applied to one of the Russia's best acting academies and was accepted out of thousands of applicants. After receiving her Master's in Arts, she was performing daily on the stages of Moscow's best and most popular theaters in front of thousands. She was welcomed into the nation's artistic and intellectual circles.

Her meteoric rise ended abruptly with the birth of her son who had a rare, incurable disease. Tatyana gave up her fairy-tale career and emigrated to the United States in order to give her son the best medical care. A complete nobody in the new world with barely any English, she held odd jobs and cared for the elderly to support her family. Her son died at nine years of age.

Tatyana had to start her life from scratch in New Jersey. She went back to school and learned computer science. A series of great corporate jobs as a programmer allowed her to move to New York City, where she also began to look for acting opportunities. Doing stand-up comedy around New York comedy clubs, she became a finalist in a Tristate Stand-Up Comedy competition. With time, she began to receive roles in television and movies and most recently, in the popular NBC series, *Chicago Fire.* She had a speaking part in the opera production, *The Nose*, by Shostakovich, at the magnificent New York Metropolitan Opera. A short film that she wrote, directed, and produced was accepted to "Short Films Corner" at the Cannes Film Festival. For three years in New York, she taught drama and creativity at the prestigious Pushkin Academy.

Tatyana believes that her ability to start her life from scratch and always succeed in things she sets her mind on is the result of Power of the Mind and Law of Attraction, which she has learned to appreciate. Willing to share her knowledge and experiences with others, she has started a production company to create educational, animated videos that would teach children and adults about the power they have inside them — the ability to create successful and joyful lives.

CHAPTER 6

IT'S NEVER TOO LATE TO MAKE A CAREER CHANGE

BY CARA HEILMANN

It starts with a nagging feeling that something isn't right. Perhaps your boss said a comment that you can't let go. Or maybe the company took a direction that left you scratching your head. You've lost the excitement, and dread settles on you like a heavy blanket. You wonder if your colleagues can see your new motto, fake it till you make it, written all over your face.

Maybe you're meant to do something else—bigger, bolder, and a bit scarier. But the prospect of losing a steady income and benefits keeps you firmly planted in a job that you could do in your sleep. Should you stay or go?

Does this sound like you? You're not alone.

I've coached over 100 clients and facilitated career transition support to over 400 job seekers—including executives, consultants, managers, and leaders—all asking for guidance on what might lie ahead, what they're meant to do. And then, once they peek at what that might be, I've helped them combat their fears of loss of income or prestige, or just the unknown.

Career changes are as varied as snowflakes. But there's a common thread weaving through the journeys of all my clients, and I'm going to share that thread with you. It all starts with slowing down, plugging in to yourself. Then becoming a scientist to research and experiment. And through it all, surviving the fear and making small and sometimes big changes in your career.

GLIMMERS

I've stopped asking young children, "What do you want to do when you grow up?" It sets the wrong expectation. According to the Federal Reserve Bank of New York, 27 percent of college graduates get a job related to their major. And researchers estimate that people change careers between one and three times before retirement. Because of this, many career assessments aren't helpful—they rely on what you are good at and omit what you want to do. In fact, I took an interest assessment that told me I should consider a career in human resources. The problem was, I was already a human resources executive—a dispirited cheerleader ready to sit out the next game.

Instead of falling back on the standard assessments, I encourage my clients to look through a keyhole to find the sparkles in life—whether at work, home, or play. Such glimmers of fullness give hints to what makes us smile and feel alive—what leaves us feeling valued, accomplished, brilliant.

This is where I believe life coaches are invaluable: we're trained to draw out stories reminding you of times when you were so very in love with your job. When you felt on top of the world. When you'd go home and tell your friends and loved ones about your amazing day. It could be a brilliant presentation. Gratitude from a colleague for making a difference. An excited email from a client. These moments connected you to something bigger—they are windows into what lights you up.

A client, a registered nurse in the military who was making the transition to the civilian world, was struggling to articulate his career achievements. When I asked about times that made him feel alive, he replied, "I set up the medical facility at a new military outpost." He shared a remarkable story: he'd estimated the number of patients that would come through the doors, projected their different ailments, determined the types of providers needed and equipment required, and then set it all in motion. At the end of six months, he orchestrated a massive effort that resulted in delivering exceptional care to hundreds at this location.

"Do you know how amazing this is?" I said. "CEOs of healthcare companies do not have this experience."

"I was just following my CO's orders," he replied. But after sitting with that moment of feeling alive, he decided to focus his civilian career on healthcare project management.

When have you felt completely alive? What was a moment that ignited your soul? That glimmer is the trailhead of an untraveled road, and just around the bend the path begins to clear. Over time, with more exposure, the vision is revealed.

Not sure what the glimmer is? Here are a few exercises to help you.

CLEAR YOUR MIND TO FIND YOUR GLIMMERS

Every runner knows—and feels—the mind-clearing effects of running. A study published in 2014 at the University of Florida showed increased activity in the brain's frontal lobe after a relatively short period of acute aerobic activity, along with improved cognitive functioning: clear thinking, planning, goal-setting, concentration, and time management. Many runners say they solve problems while in motion.

Running not your thing? Similar acute aerobic activity, like thirty to forty minutes of a vigorous workout that makes you sweat, provides the same mind-clearing effects. Jump on the stationary bike, go for a brisk walk or a swim, lift weights, or do other muscle-strengthening activities of moderate to high intensity levels that meet your abilities: the main goal is to get that heart rate pumping.

Then sit in your favorite spot, relax, and grab your journal, notepad, tablet, or laptop. Jot down your thoughts to these questions:

- *Looking back at your career, where were you when you felt the most alive? What were you doing? Who was around you? What was your impact on them?*
- *If you created a billboard that ten thousand people passed every day, what would it say or show? What values have you honored?*
- *In your last role, what are successes that your company valued? What are successes that you valued?*

- *If you could do anything, what would that look like?*
- *Think about what excites you most. What would need to be here, right now, to have that aliveness in your life?*

This journaling may take several sittings. Do you need more space to reflect? Go on a retreat—a period of quiet reflection in a safe environment. This could be a garden, a beach, a park bench. Or, if you have the time and resources, you can spend a day or more at a nearby retreat center.

A former colleague calls this **sitting on the rock**: giving yourself breathing room to reflect, think, ponder, and plan. When you are done sitting on the rock, read over your answers. Ask yourself, what are the common threads?

Once you've identified a glimmer, see what about it is right for you. Experiment with different roles and immerse yourself in the glimmer.

TRY THE GLIMMER ON FOR SIZE

A client convinced that working for a nonprofit was a glimmer. Her coach recommended that she spend a day or two at a nonprofit conference talking to people in the field. Upon her return, she said she'd connected with incredible people doing incredible things. And had a surprising epiphany—she left with the certainty that she didn't want to work for a small community nonprofit because of the intense focus on fund-raising. She then turned to social enterprises working in areas of great interest to her.

Here are a few ways you can try something on before you make a commitment to leave your current employment situation:

- *Rewrite your résumé as if you were applying for a position touching on your glimmer.*
- *Attend a conference, and ask participants what they love and dislike about the field.*
- *Find a professional association that has regular meetings, and ask to be a guest.*
- *Locate an employee at a company you'd like to work for, and ask them out to lunch to chat about their experience.*

- *Find someone who is doing the type of work you wish to do, and request a short telephone appointment to learn more about their job.*
- *Reach out to an entrepreneur in your targeted role or industry. Ask them how they decided to open their business and if they have any regrets. Write a business plan as if you were to open a similar company.*
- *Take a class or read an industry journal to learn more about the field.*
- *Research job postings with tasks that seem to touch on your glimmer.*
- *Take a temporary job or side gig in the targeted role, industry, or company.*

A word of caution: the informational conversations you'll have in your career exploration are not the time to sell yourself or pass along your résumé. When we walk into a conversation to sell, we can't suppress this agenda—it will leak through our expressions and tone of voice. Your intention should be one of learning, curiosity, examining, educating you on the glimmer. To identify what you like and, just as importantly, what you don't like.

Now is the time to act. Researching hours on end on the internet doesn't engage all of you—reach out, talk to people, attend events. There is power in moving forward. It's physics—Newton's Law in action. As you continue to move toward your dream, trust that the path will unfold.

TAKE DIRECTIONALLY CORRECT STEPS

Rarely do we step into exactly what we're meant to do. Often, we make directionally correct moves: small changes to our career that can result in meaningful differences in our overall job satisfaction. Taking these small steps over time requires us to be open to some level of inaccuracy.

A client with a job in sales leadership lands on the belief that he wants to start his own business providing one-on-one coaching to sales professionals. He decides to make a small pivot in his career that is directionally correct, and he accepts a job as a sales trainer for a global company. His goal is to stay in this role for a few years, obtain his coaching certification, and apply his new expertise to the people he will be training.

What's interesting is that people sometimes make these moves without realizing it. A client takes a risk, leaves a corporate job, and accepts a contract position with a startup. Within a year, the startup runs out of money, and the client is convinced she made a mistake. She quickly accepts a role helping a four star hotel shut its doors. She later pivots and launches a company in the outplacement field using what she had learned from the startup. Looking back, she realizes that there was something attractive about the startup—a glimmer instrumental to where she is today. If she hadn't followed that hunch, she'd still be unhappy in a corporate job.

Career moves that seem to be mistakes may pay off later—sometimes we just don't see the connection today. Don't be afraid to pivot.

SIT IN THE FEAR

Too often we let fear rule. When faced with an opportunity to do something big, our amygdala goes into hyperdrive: this is the same tiny, yet persistent voice that warned us as four-year-olds not to run across the street without holding an adult's hand. And as we became adults, our amygdala warned about other risks, like volunteering for new assignments or a promotion. Deep down, it wants to keep us safe, so it stops us from taking steps in directions that could unleash our best selves.

When I ask my clients to think about the things they most want to do, I hear descriptors like "scary" and "exciting." One described it as standing at the edge of a cliff with his friends down below, hooting at him to jump into the water. What is my recommendation when I hear the excitement and vibrancy in their voices? Jump.

Making small and big changes to your career can feel very threatening. But like the client with the startup experience, all that you've done is part of you—you're not really starting from scratch.

Sit in the fear. Know what fear feels like. I lead clients through a meditation to find out what it might be saying. One client considering a major career change begins to cry. The fear rests in her chest, her heart is beating wildly. I ask her, "What is it telling you?"

She pauses and says, "Find yourself. Love something passionately."

Our bodies are amazing and when we listen, they tell us remarkable things. Here are a few things you can do to recognize the voice of your fear, sit with it, and guide yourself out:

- **Name the fear**. In your journal, answer these questions: what are you afraid of? What are you lacking? What is your fear telling you? Once you name it, it will lose some of its power to hold you back.
- **Thank your fear**. Acknowledge your amygdala for doing its job to keep you safe. Then rewrite its job description—demote it from the Chief Safety Officer to the Safety Assistant.
- **Quiet negative chatter**. Meditate. Pray. Read books on quieting the mind. The Power of Now by Eckart Tolle is one of the most influential books I've read in a very long time.
- **Face your fear**. **And do it again**. Challenged by her coach to face a fear, a client asked a colleague (whom she disliked for months) to lunch. Feeling emboldened, she decided to do something she's been wanting to do for about a year, she asked for a raise. Now she is considering opening her own consulting business. When you face fear once, you know you can do it. And then do it again.

KEEP LEARNING

It's never too late to make a change. I've seen this again and again over the years with clients who've found the courage to shift to their dream careers.

Armed with a degree in public policy and a heart to serve, a client became a police officer and spent his free time volunteering at a temple working as a youth advisor. He fell in love with congregation life and became a rabbi where he served for 30 years. Today, he is excited at the opportunity to lead a non-profit collaborating with community leaders to build religious inclusion in neighborhoods.

What looked like career mistakes were actually turns aligned with his glimmers of addressing public needs and building communities of faith. During our coaching session he said, "Looking back at my life, I can see that it all makes sense."

U-turns in your career don't need to be failures. You can view each situation, each move as part of a purpose. You are learning something new with every step you take in your career transition. Explore the glimmers, because you're meant to step out and do great things. Open that business, take that promotion, jump into a completely different line of work. It's never too late. And in fact, the timing is perfect.

About Cara

Born into a hardworking middle-class family in Aiea, Hawaii, Cara Heilmann knows the value of a strong work ethic as she worked in her family's manufacturing business throughout her childhood. Years later, when her father landed in the emergency room, Cara blanched at her desk-bound life and translated that work ethic to becoming a runner. Since then, she has run countless half-marathons, three full marathons, and several 24-hour relay races. Cara carries this grit and determination to her professional life as well.

Cara has worked for large Fortune 500 organizations—Kaiser Permanente®, ARAMARK, Baxter Healthcare—and medium to small organizations—AMN Healthcare®, Clinical Laboratories of Hawaii, Vantaggio HR. After a long career in executive recruiting and Human Resources, Cara is now CEO of Ready Reset Go™, a career-coaching company helping people find jobs that ignite their hearts. Her clients range from physicians to new graduates to CEOs. Her greatest joy is hearing clients say, "I got the job!"

Cara is a recognized expert, speaker, and trainer and has taught on today's job search methods, uncovering unconscious biases, giving and getting feedback, recruiting search techniques, and improv interviewing preparation.

Cara is very involved in the community as a member of the Board of Directors of Wardrobe for Opportunity, a nonprofit in Oakland ending poverty by helping individuals get a job, keep a job, and build a career.

Cara has a Master of Business Administration from Vanderbilt University and a Bachelor of Business Administration from the University of Hawaii at Manoa. She is a certified Senior Professional Human Resources, a Certified Professional Résumé Writer, a Certified Professional Career Coach, and a member of the Forbes Coaches Council. She is also certified in the Lominger Recruiting Architect® and TRACOM® Group Social Styles.

Cara resides in the San Francisco Bay Area with her husband and two boys where she runs throughout the East Bay Hills.

Cara loves to hear from people, feel free to connect:
- www.linkedin.com/in/caraheilmann/
- www.readyresetgo.com
- @CaraHeilmann

CHAPTER 7

TRANSFORM STRATEGY TO ACTION
PREPARING FOR SUCCESS

BY CHERYL WHEELER, CMC

Quality is never an accident. It is always the result of intelligent effort.
~ John Ruskin – leading English art critic of the Victorian era

You are an executive or entrepreneur from the turbulent world of business. You may oversee a complex operation, or you're looking to make your business dream a reality. You strive every day to deliver the promised customer experience all while relentlessly navigating the ever-shifting digital business landscape. You may also have C-suite accountability to investors and directors for profitable growth, increased market share, and sustainable value creation. This is your reality.

Whoever you are, you're under constant pressure to control costs, increase productivity, and focus on operational effort and capital investment that optimizes performance and delivers measurable results. Your solid grounding in business tells you that success rarely comes from some trendy app, or from the introduction of a cool, new approach. You get that in the real world, there are no silver bullets.

You're aware that no prototype of an aircraft ever took off from Boeing Field and remained aloft with a long-term return on investment (ROI), based on a plan-on-a-page, cute Prezi animation, and nonexistent production designs.

71

You know that, *in the real world, achieving real success takes real commitment!*

"Nearly 60 percent of projects failed to fully meet their objectives: 44 percent missed at least one time, budget or quality goal, while a full 15 percent either missed all goals or were stopped by management." [1]

Surely, in the nearly ten years since the above study was conducted, one would expect that we've cracked the code and are no longer failing so miserably. There are countless books, articles and best-practice approaches that have been developed to avoid risks associated with business start-up or transformation, as well as numerous consulting firms professing their expertise in the same.

Sadly, I wish I could say that businesses are no longer making the same mistakes, particularly at a time when they are amid significant digital transformations.

As millennials (and even some of us baby boomers) charge forward in a digital world, we are compelled by our personal experiences as we use digital technology as part of our day-to-day lives. As a result, our expectations as consumers have radically changed. Businesses must be positioned to respond to these growing expectations or risk obsolescence.

According to a study conducted in 2013 involving over 1,500 executives in 106 countries [2]:

> *"78% say digital transformation will become critical to their organizations within the next two years."*

Therefore, one might suggest that if your business hasn't already embarked on a significant digital transformation initiative and pulled it off, you're at risk of missing the boat altogether. Further to that study...

> *"81% of people believe digital transformation will give their company a competitive advantage."*

So, given that your business' competitive advantage and perhaps even its very survival is dependent on your digital transformation being successful, we better start getting it right.

Unfortunate Reality

Sadly, over my 25+ year career, I've seen numerous examples of failures – so many in fact, that a significant aspect of my career involved transformation rescue. Whether the goal was a simple realignment of an organizational structure to drive out efficiency or a large-scale, enterprise-wide transformation of people, process, information and technology, the story was the same.

One example of this was a large organization who, for more than a decade, attempted to automate their outdated registration and scheduling system. In fact, they purchased three completely different software solutions and failed to implement the first two which cost the organization millions of dollars. It was amidst their third attempt that I got called in to complete a risk assessment on their failing transformation and develop a plan to get it back on track. Given the organization's previous failed attempts, the massive investment already down the drain, the Board was very concerned that the transformation initiative was off the rails – again.

As with nearly all my transformation rescues, my findings were the same. With my remediation plan in hand, I was engaged by the organization to get their transformation back on track and take it to the finish line – and I did just that, in less than six months!

How was this accomplished?

1. Ensure unwavering leadership commitment

Desire is the key to motivation, but it's determination and commitment to an unrelenting pursuit of your goal - a commitment to excellence - that will enable you to attain the success you seek.
~ Mario Andretti, Italian-born American former racing driver

It's imperative that leadership plays an active role and is viewed as supportive of the transformation.

The organization's leadership team was engaged and intimately involved in the definition of the vision and outcomes, and high-level planning. As a result, the value became clear in their minds, and critical business staff were mobilized to support the transformation efforts – providing support from the side of their desks does not work.

2. Clear vision and measurable results

Good business leaders create a vision, articulate the vision, passionately own the vision, and relentlessly drive it to completion.
~ Jack Welch, former chairman and CEO of General Electric

It is critical to have a clear vision and a definition of outcomes that are meaningful and measurable – a North Star aiming point for sustainable success.

Many organizations go through the motions of defining outcomes and come up with outcome statements such as "Organizational Excellence" or "Empowered Staff". These are motherhood statements that are virtually meaningless and certainly not measurable.

Key members of the organization (including the leadership team) developed measurable outcomes through facilitated sessions. They were developed based on the identified needs and expectations of stakeholders (customers, investors, partners, suppliers, employees, and communities-of-interest). These new outcomes were clear, meaningful, measurable, and in terms that the stakeholders could relate to – responding to the "what's-in-it-for-me" statement.

The result was that the leadership and stakeholders were passionate about their North Star. They believed that achieving these outcomes was critical to the success of their transformation as well as their success.

3. Adoption planning (organizational change management)

It may be hard for an egg to turn into a bird: it would be a jolly sight harder for it to learn to fly while remaining an egg.
~ C. S. Lewis, British novelist

As with most transformation failures, it's rare that the technology was at the root of the problem – although it's usually to blame. It's typically the people side of the change that was not appropriately planned for or managed well. Even though it is now best practice to embed stakeholder engagement, communications, training and knowledge transfer practices and activities in a transformation initiative, it is still often overlooked.

To prepare for their transformation, I conducted a readiness assessment. It consisted of a high-level scan of staff and other key stakeholders to assess: if stakeholders understood the vision and case for change; whether they had a positive view; and their perceptions of the organization's change readiness strengths and constraints. The results of the scan were used to inform an adoption strategy which defined the approaches to engagement, communication, consultation, training, knowledge transfer and feedback mechanisms.

4. Clear and correct design of the future-state business

Details create the big picture.
~ Sanford I. Weill, American banker, financier and philanthropist

The creation of the definition and design of the future-state business ensures that complex needs are understood. Without this, it would be like attempting to put together a complex puzzle without the benefit of the picture on the box. You would be unable to confirm if the individual pieces you are trying to put together will result in the correct image.

Designing the future business solution takes effort. It takes people – executives and staff alike.

It is crucial to involve employees (internal to the organization) who have the depth and breadth of knowledge of the business area(s) that are the subject of transformation. It also requires individuals with specialized skills in project management, business design, business analysis, change management, and technology.

A team of external consultants was brought in to provide support for workshops and conduct in-depth reviews of business activities to develop the future-state business design, and determine if the current capabilities meet stakeholder needs (and if not, ascertained what needed to change).

Additionally, a working committee was engaged to provide business-specific expertise during workshops and interviews. This committee included staff from each of the impacted business areas. It also included a mixture of staff that represented the distinct organizational levels comprising of leadership and day-to-day, hands-on support staff.

The designs of the future-state business included business processes, policies, business rules and decision models, business organization structure, and information and technology models.

With the concise picture of their future-state in hand, they had no trouble mapping out a clear path forward to achieve their vision.

My Next Plan of Attack

Whether trying to get their businesses off the ground or embarking on a large-scale transformation, I recognized that the issues my clients experienced were essentially the same.

Disenchanted from more than a decade of rescuing transformations, I decided to no longer pursue this line of work, and I took off for the beaches of Spain to recover myself. I read the book, *Change Your Thinking, Change Your Life: How to Unlock Your Full Potential.*[3] I guess it was time for my transformation! After a month of self-discovery, I felt fully rejuvenated and had determined my next plan of attack.

Getting involved at the beginning, I was confident that I could prevent transformation failure from happening in the first place. That became my new focus.

I immediately took a 4-month sabbatical from client work and, inspired by my successes (and lessons learned), created a methodology that would assure the success of any business transformation from a business start-up to organizational restructuring and large-scale digital transformation. And so, Transform Strategy to Action™ (or TS2A™) was born. TS2A™ establishes the keys to success and ensures that businesses are ready <u>before</u> commencing on a transformational journey.

> *And will you succeed? Yes, you will indeed!*
> *(98 and 3/4 percent guaranteed.)*
> ~ Dr. Seuss, American author

TS2A™ focuses on four main categories which address the issues typically faced by organizations in their attempts to transform:

1. Strategic Intent
2. Business Definition and Design
3. Transformation Readiness
4. Transformation Plan and Roadmap

I have substantially mitigated the risks and issues my clients typically encounter and positioned them to embark on successful transformation journeys attaining real, measurable results. Positioning for success is accomplished by ensuring that leadership is fully committed, the right internal business resources are mobilized, the specialized subject matter experts are in place, and, by following the TS2A™ steps (shown in Table 1).

	TS2A™ Component	Description of Effort	Resulting Success Enablers
Strategic Intent	Vision and Outcomes	Define outcomes and measures based on stakeholders needs. Based on the outcomes and measures, create a Business Context Model to illustrate the subject of transformation (high-level business scope).	• Strategic Outcomes – "North Star" • Business Outcomes and Measures • Business Context Model
Future-State Business Definition and Design	Business Solution Concept	Define the ideal-state processes, information model and technical capabilities. Combine with stakeholder needs and outcomes to create the Business Solution Concept.	• Business Service and Process Model • Process Value Assessment • Capabilities List • Information Model • Technical Architecture Model • Business Solution Concept
	Business Blueprint	Design the future-state business solution including process, organization, data, and technical designs as well as identify policies, business rules, and decision models.	• End-to-End Process Designs • Process Risks and Controls Assessments • Business Organization Design • Policy, Rules and Decision Models • Logical Data Model • Technology Platform

Transformation Readiness	Transformation Readiness	Create an Implementation Strategy and identify Success Principles based on an assessment of change readiness (capacity, culture, commitment) and financial feasibility. Define governance and organization structure. Determine project management approach (waterfall or agile).	• Adoption Strategy • Transformation Governance & Organization Structure • Funding Framework • Implementation Strategy • Success Principles • Project Management Approach
	Transformation Preparation	Develop communication and change management plans. Onboard transformation support and project or sprint teams. Conduct project approach and platform overview training. Conduct Security Threat Risk and Privacy Impact Assessments. Configure platform to support core functionality.	• Communication and Change Plans • Transformation Support and Project Teams • Preparation Training • Technical Platform Assessments • Core Platform Functionality
Transformation Plan and Roadmap	Transformation Plan	Identify solutions to address the root cause of prioritized capability gaps. Consolidate solutions to form the basis of an Initiative List or Product Backlog. Assess feasibility of decommissioning legacy systems (if applicable). Develop Benefits Realization Plan based on Outcomes & Measures.	• Capability Value and Gap Assessment • Root Cause Analysis • Initiative List or Product Backlog • System Decommissioning Feasibility • Benefits Realization Plan
	Transformation Roadmap	Estimate cost and duration of Initiatives or Product Backlog items. Group items into Releases based on organizational change impact (implementation feasibility), and system decommissioning feasibility.	• Initiative or Product Backlog Estimates • Release Definition • Transformation Roadmap

Table 1: TS2A™ Methodology[4]

Proven Success

In recent years, my team and I have applied T2SA™ with proven success in a broad range of sectors: transportation, healthcare, consumer product, banking, and government.

For the 17th largest transit company in North America, we helped to conceive, plan and successfully execute an Enterprise Investment Initiative (EII) that far-and-away exceeded all client expectations. The COO told us that "because of your unique approach to identifying investments that deliver real value, our company spent a bit of money resolving our many business problems, instead of millions of dollars automating them." Our efforts helped his C-suite team to increase ridership; optimize the customer experience; reduce costs; repair strained partner and union relationships; increase employee satisfaction and fortify the financial sustainability of his company.

For the third largest provincial government in Canada, we developed an elaborate suite of business designs and process optimization strategies. Our client was positioned to realize their goals to optimize road safety and increase access to timely and fair dispute resolution options for 4.6 million citizens, generate millions of dollars in avoided costs related to healthcare and policing and, enhance public trust and confidence in their government.

It is not the strongest of the species that survives, nor the most intelligent that survives. It is the one that is the most adaptable to change.
~ Charles Darwin, English naturalist, geologist and biologist

---

1. IBM Global CEO Study (2008)
2. Cap Gemini and MIT Sloan Management Review
3. *Change Your Thinking, Change Your Life: How to Unlock Your Full Potential,* by Brian Tracy
4. Mejora Consulting Inc., All rights reserved

About Cheryl

Cheryl Wheeler is an inspiring and results-oriented business design and transformation specialist. Ensuring alignment and traceability of actions and investments to business strategies is her passion.

Cheryl grew up in Vancouver, British Columbia, Canada. Driven to get on with life, Cheryl married young and started out her adult life as a stay-at-home Mom. As with the typical challenges faced by marrying so young, a few years later, Cheryl found herself a single parent. Challenged to make ends meet, she quit her job as a file clerk, took out a student loan, and went back to school. She enrolled in the Accelerated Computers Systems Management program at Capilano University in Vancouver where she graduated with honors in 1990.

Armed with new knowledge and bursting with confidence, she took the information technology world by storm and quickly progressed from network support specialist in an engineering company to the Director of Outsourcing for CGI (Canada's largest IT outsourcing firm), and Account Executive for Cap Gemini Consulting.

After expanding her breadth and depth of knowledge and expertise in management consulting, outsourcing, and business transformation, Cheryl's goal was to create a reliable, economical alternative to the consulting firms who overwhelm and overbill with unnecessary complexity. A true entrepreneur by nature, Cheryl gave up the corporate world and, in 2006, founded Mejora Consulting Inc.

Under Cheryl's thought leadership, Mejora has perfected practical approaches to strategic planning, business design and enterprise business architecture, business process optimization, and business transformation.

Cheryl spent a large part of her 25-year career rescuing failing projects and restoring client confidence through well-managed and well-executed engagements. Based on this experience, she created Transform Strategy to Action™, (or TS2A™). This robust methodology examines those areas of the business where there may be misalignment to strategic outcomes and targets – such as policy, organizational structure, people capability and capacity, business processes, infrastructure, and information systems and enabling technologies.

It is suggested that she is the first practitioner on the planet to crack the code on how to sensibly embrace, but not overly engineer the very best aspects of new Agile thinking by adapting TS2A™ to create TS2A - Agile Transformation™.

Over at Mejora, her team views Cheryl as being an impressive entrepreneur, a passionate perfectionist, and a truly authentic natural leader of people.

Cheryl is now focusing on taking Mejora to a new level in assisting clients to achieve long-term and sustainable success. Cheryl will continue to perfect and deliver world-class consulting and training services and is also in the process of providing TS2A™ online in the form of toolkits which include clear, step-by-step instructions, tips and tricks, templates, and instructional videos. Cheryl's goal is for her clients to build internal business capability and workforce capacity, and avoid becoming ever-dependent on self-focused consultants.

Cheryl recently moved to a stunning ocean-front home in Victoria, British Columbia – proof that TS2A works. In addition to applying TS2A to Mejora's transformation, Cheryl applied the same concepts to her personal transformation.

If you'd like to learn more, please do not hesitate to contact Cheryl at:
- cheryl.wheeler@mejora.ca
- https://www.linkedin.com/in/cheryl-wheeler-18180316/
- 1-604-351-1077
- www.mejora.ca
- https://twitter.com/Mejora_TS2A

CHAPTER 8

HOW TO SET AND ACHIEVE GOALS WITH I.M.P.A.C.T.

BY ELLEN McNEILL, CMSC, CGSC, CMC, CSFC, CPC

A study conducted by Harvard indicates that 83% of the U.S. population do not have goals. I was one of them. That was until 1989.

I was listening to a motivational tape by Tony Robbins when it struck me. What was I doing with my life? I had friends, close family ties, a job, no financial worries, but I felt something was missing. It was a sense of accomplishment. That is when I decided to turn an idea to invent a product, and have it featured on Home Shopping Network (HSN), into an actionable goal.

I drew some sketches of a design for a "hanging" jewelry organizer and created several different prototypes until I found one I was happy with. (This was over thirty years ago, so hanging organizers weren't yet commonplace).

A local mother-daughter team manufactured the organizer for me.

Now I needed packaging, so I hired a package design firm. Working closely with a designer, we created eye-catching packaging for the organizer.

Only one task remained – how to get the finished product in front of the HSN buyers. Getting appointments with them was almost impossible unless you were a household name. The only place my name was a household name was in my own household.

I watched HSN and noticed a personal trainer who was very popular. He was frequently on-air offering a variety of training products. I boldly called his office to determine if he would present the organizer to HSN buyers on my behalf. We set up a meeting and he graciously said he would. I was ecstatic. I was sure the HSN buyers would love the organizer as much as I did and want to put it on-air.

The big presentation day came . . . and went. HSN decided not to accept my organizer.

At first blush this may seem to be a "goal failure" story. It isn't. I learned early on that something is only a "failure" if you don't gain knowledge and grow from it. I don't regret my HSN adventure because I learned:

1. How to set goals and take directed and focused action.
2. That I could design a product from merely a thought, create a prototype and have it made into a product for mass market.
3. How to source a product's components and find a manufacturer to produce it.
4. That I was creative.
5. That I could contribute to package design for a product.
6. How to write marketing copy for product packaging.
7. That I had the courage to contact a famous person and convince him to meet with me face-to-face.
8. That my organizer could get to the point where it would actually be shown to HSN buyers.
9. To do market research first to determine if there is a problem for which women are seeking a solution.
10. That I could write a design patent application and learn how to submit it for registration (I had an attorney review it).
11. That I could deal with a major disappointment and not merely GO through it, but GROW through it.
12. That I didn't know what I didn't know.

Besides these 12 valuable, life-changing lessons, I did have a major accomplishment that I didn't anticipate. I was issued three U.S. patents on my jewelry organizer designs.

Another valuable lesson? Having goals are essential to success in life.

WHY SET GOALS ANYWAY?

1. **CHOICE VERSUS "COASTING":** Without goals to strive for, you'll coast through life living at the result of whatever life brings your way. I was coasting before I set the goal to create a product and market it through HSN. I made a conscious decision to stop letting life HAPPEN TO ME and to start MAKING THINGS HAPPEN in my life instead.

2. **FOCUS:** Goals provide focus and forward direction. They unleash razor sharp "mind power" and can help you feel happier. Once you set a goal it becomes "top of mind". You'll automatically compare tasks on your TO-DO list to your goal to determine what to do next and what not to do.

3. **CLARITY AND MEANING:** Goals bring a sense of simplicity and purpose to life. Your path to a future long-term goal will become visible. Mental "fogginess" will disappear and be replaced with a richer sense of perspective.

4. **STRUCTURE:** Many of us lack any real structure in our lives. Our "structure" – the "BIG PICTURE" of our lives – can easily become distorted by myriad tasks, interruptions and "stuff" that loudly demands our attention. Having goals will enable you to get back to the "BIG PICTURE" quickly after an interruption or distraction.

WHAT YOU NEED TO KNOW BEFORE SETTING GOALS

1. **WRITE YOUR GOALS DOWN!** Avoid just THINKING about setting goals and not doing anything else about them. Writing your goals down, and sharing them with someone who has confidence in you, makes them more concrete and motivating. It's important to actually WRITE your goals down rather than typing them or using a notetaking app. The mere act of writing your goals down increases the odds of you accomplishing your goals by 42%, according to a study done by Dr. Gail Matthew, psychology professor at Dominican University of Florida.

2. **GOALS REQUIRE TIME, EFFORT AND RESOURCES TO ACCOMPLISH:** Because we can imagine a goal – which makes

it real to us – we can tend to gloss over the details and process that will be involved in accomplishing it. The pace of a high-tech society has led many of us to shift from expecting "instant gratification" to expecting "instant results." We even get impatient when the driver in front of us takes an extra three seconds to hit the gas. Setting a goal doesn't get you from "think to blink" where the achievement appears in the blink of an eye. Be prepared to invest a lot of time and put forth genuine effort. "Trying" isn't going to cut it.

3. **A "STRAIGHT LINE GOAL PATH" IS AN ILLUSION:** When we set a goal, we expect that the path to achievement will be straightforward, going directly from "A" to "B". The reality is that the road to accomplishment is more like a winding road with many curves. The road will curve right, left, lead to other roads and change into yet another road. Accept that the "Straight Line Goal Path" does not exist. If you don't, you will experience disappointment and frustration when a setback occurs or an obstacle appears.

4. **CHANGE IS GOING TO COME:** Answer the following question before you set a goal, "Am I willing to do things differently, totally change habits and routines, and make sacrifices and tradeoffs in order to accomplish my goal?" Anything new that you move forward on in life or business, including setting goals, will require that changes be made somewhere. A common response to change is "resistance." You may experience this as well even if YOU set the goal that caused the change. That's because the world will change around you as you change. Keep moving forward and be prepared for unanticipated and surprising changes. Carl Jung, founder of analytical psychology, brilliantly said, "What you resist persists."

THE I.M.P.A.C.T. GOAL SETTING APPROACH

Looking back on my first goal setting adventure – creating a product and getting it in front of HSN buyers – I realized that I was unknowingly following certain steps to set, and get, my goal.

Analyzing those steps led to development of the I.M.P.A.C.T. approach to goal setting. These six steps will help you set and get your goals while encouraging and motivating you at the same time. I.M.P.A.C.T. represents:

1. **I**NTENTION
2. **M**EASURABLE
3. **P**OWERFUL
4. **A**CTIONABLE
5. **C**OMPELLING
6. **T**IMED

The steps overlap and work together to provide a success-oriented framework for setting and achieving goals. Here they are:

1. INTENTION

An INTENTION is your overarching, broad statement of a vision, dream or idea. For a business, it is a "rough target" or "aim" a company considers such as increasing annual revenue.

THINKING ABOUT >>>> **DECISION** >>>> **TAKING ACTION**

>_____>

INTENTION >> **TRANSFORM** >> **GOAL**

Making the decision to shape your INTENTION into a goal, puts the vision, dream or idea into "action mode". There is now an opportunity to transform your INTENTION into a reality.

When setting a goal, do not use non-powerful words like "WANT" or be vague or general. Thinking – "We want to increase our business income over the next three years." – is not a goal. It's merely a statement and a wish.

A goal must be positive, well-defined and stated clearly with as much precision as possible. Here's the "thought" above worded perfectly as a precise goal that can be easily communicated and understood:

"The Company's goal is that we WILL increase our current annual sales as of (current date) by 50%, by the end of the 36th month from (current date)."

The goal now includes all of the information requested throughout the six steps of the I.M.P.A.C.T. method. It provides direction for the company and its team members, is not vague or general, and states "WILL" versus "WANT".

2. MEASURABLE

Awareness of whether or not you are making headway on your goal is critical. Tracking and measuring progress will provide that information. It's also a form of accountability for yourself and your team members.

Begin the measuring process by asking, "How will I measure progress on my goal?" The measuring criterion should be objective, meaningful and quantifiable.

Progress on the three-year sales goal cited above can be easily measured in dollars and percentages based on how the goal is worded.

Reports on advancement of the goal should be reviewed frequently to determine if:

    a. The Company is meeting its target numbers.
    b. Something has occurred to impede progress.
    c. The goal is in a "holding pattern."
    d. Something unexpected has happened.

You can track progress annually, monthly or weekly because the goal as stated breaks down to a rounded percentage increase of:

    ➢ 17% annually
    ➢ 1.40% monthly
    ➢ 0.35% weekly

If you are not satisfied with progress at any given point, identify what is affecting the results. This will enable you to fix the problem before it becomes unmanageable. Without progress reports, a problem can balloon out of control and derail accomplishment of the goal.

3. POWERFUL

To set a POWERFUL goal the first thing you need to change is your belief in yourself and your team.

Many goal setting models suggest setting goals that are "realistic" and "attainable" so you will not be disappointed if you don't achieve them. Who is to say what is "realistic" or "attainable" for you? No one but you can know what you or your company are capable of when you all have focus and direction.

"Uplevel" a previous goal you have set. Set a goal that pushes your limits. A POWERFUL goal forces you to increase your knowledge and sometimes take quantum leaps. You may not be sure exactly HOW the goal will be accomplished. You just know that it will.

We each have skills and know-hows that come naturally to us or that we have learned and developed over the years. We don't necessarily use all of them every day so we are not consciously aware of all of them until they appear. Determine what skills and competencies you and your team may need to acquire to accomplish your goal and get training that will move the goal forward.

Your POWERFUL goal should be demanding but without many seemingly impassible obstacles to work through. That could easily lead to demotivation and giving up on your goal.

The results you are seeking, and the process you follow, must be in alignment with your core values and belief systems. If not, you will experience internal conflict that could interfere with accomplishment of your goal.

4. ACTIONABLE

Any goal you set should be ACTIONABLE and lead to a comprehensive, consistent and in-depth ACTION PLAN. Major tasks, short-term goals and significant milestones required to achieve your goal should be included.

All daily tasks and activities must move goal accomplishment forward in some way. Every daily TO-DO list should include 1-2 contributing steps.

Current resources will need to be assessed to determine if improvements or additional resources are required. The ACTION PLAN will also define the key results areas that will be impacted by your goal.

Efficient and effective morning routines – at home and in the office— combined with daily tasks and activities completed – will make the difference between goal accomplishment and failure.

An ACTION PLAN should be flexible and adaptable to unexpected circumstances.

These are just some of factors to take into account when crafting an ACTION PLAN.

5. COMPELLING

We don't usually consider if our goal is COMPELLING, exciting and interesting enough to pursue. It may be exhilarating at first but lack potential for long-term interest. An uninspiring goal will curtail perseverance through setbacks or roadblocks. A COMPELLING goal sustains motivation and keeps momentum going.

Keep the "BIG PICTURE" of your goal "top of mind". It can help your goal remain COMPELLING over the long-term because you'll continually reconnect with the goal's initial excitement. Overlooking the "BIG PICTURE" can drag you down when faced with an unpleasant or boring task.

A COMPELLING goal should be challenging and aggressive enough to maintain interest in moving forward but not so frustrating that you are tempted to quit. Plan your strategies for staying motivated and excited during the "goal-getting" process beforehand. Take into account that unforeseen circumstances will occur. Some may set you back. Some will catapult you forward. Be prepared.

A strong support system will help you stay motivated and COMPELLED to accomplish your goal. Even a quick e-mail, text or telephone call to a friend can make a difference in your outlook. Spend the majority of your time with goal setters and goal getters and avoid naysayers.

6. TIMED

Your POWERFUL goal must have a precise start and end date to guide you to accomplishing it. "BY WHEN EXACTLY?" provides you and your team with a structural framework to lead you through the other steps in the I.M.P.A.C.T. approach.

Once the timeline is set, short-term goals can be identified, prioritized and milestones determined.

Think about this. If you were to merely answer an end date question with "by the end of next year" it's ambiguous. Your answer could mean the end of October, the end of November, the end of December or the end of the fiscal year. This demonstrates why a precise timeline is important. It directly affects how tasks, activities, short-term goals and milestones get scheduled in the ACTION PLAN, and when they should be completed.

The process of achieving your goal will be a hands-on learning experience. I can say that without a doubt. It will create fulfillment or an emotional drain depending on your outlook about the process, your willingness to work and your perspective.

Approach goal setting, and the process, with enthusiasm, a positive attitude and an open mind.

My goal for you? Become a businesswoman who accomplishes her goals with knowledge gained and a sense of personal satisfaction.

Today's actions are the seeds of tomorrow's results.
~ Ellen McNeill

About Ellen

As a **Mindset Expert Specializing in Goal Achievement and Motivation**, Ellen McNeill, CEO of Mindset Coaching Institute LLC, works with women entrepreneurs to help them (1) finally achieve their goals, (2) maintain their motivation through setbacks and obstacles, (3) optimize their resources to achieve the greatest results possible and much, much more.

You may wonder, "Why get coaching on my mindset?" For one simple reason – **your mindset is everything**. Why does Ellen say that? Because everywhere you go, there you are. You bring your mindset, attitude, beliefs, viewpoints, agenda—everything—with you. Sometimes it works in your favor in your business. Sometimes it doesn't. That's why working on your mindset is so important.

Ellen's signature coaching program – **The Mindset Factor – Mastering the Key to Your Ultimate Success** – provides a comprehensive approach to help you as you work the steps to accomplish each milestone on your path towards your ultimate goal – achieving your vision.

Ellen's credentials and more than 35 years of business experience, combined with her natural analytical skills and friendly results-oriented style, make her a valuable asset and resource for your business and your life. She specializes in helping Women Entrepreneurs achieve the tangible bottom line results they are looking for to grow their businesses and achieve the goals they truly desire.

Meeting her own goals to support and serve her clients in reaching the results they desire, Ellen has earned five distinct accreditations:

- Certified Mind Set Coach
- Certified Goal Setting Coach
- Certified Motivation Coach
- Certified Solution-Focused Coach
- Certified Life Coach

What do these five certifications mean to you? They mean that Ellen has received training that makes her well-rounded and capable of coaching you in all the critical areas that can help you achieve the business and lifestyle results that are important to you.

Ellen is well-known for having an uncanny ability to "see what's invisible" to you as an entrepreneur. Discovering your "blind spots" will enable you, working with

Ellen as your Mindset Coach, to identify opportunities that are slipping through your fingers. Revealing "blind spots" can also help you dissolve perceived roadblocks and obstacles with ease.

She was a motivational speaker for six years, speaking to business professionals across a broad spectrum of more than 20 different industries. She offered unique insights into stepping up productivity, systematizing goal setting and practicing effective time management.

Ellen Martorella (McNeill) is listed in the Yearbook of Experts, Authorities and Spokespersons, 12th Edition, as an expert on Productivity and Motivation and is a Member of the National Association of Experts, Writers & Speakers (2017).

Dubbed a "productivity guru" by the University of South Florida Small Business Development Center in Tampa, Florida, Ellen is a dynamic, thought-provoking speaker, published author and television personality.

She was also an instructor specializing in time management and organizational skills at St. Petersburg Junior College in St. Petersburg, Florida.

Ellen is very creative in her approach to life and business as evidenced by three U.S. Patents she was issued on a product she designed, developed and brought to market.

To connect with Ellen:
- www.ellenmcneill.com
- www.linkedin.com/in/EllenMcNeill
- www.facebook.com/EllenMcNeillCoachingForWomenEntrepreneurs

CHAPTER 9

STEP INTO WELLNESS AND PERSONAL GROWTH

BY JOE MORIARTY

THE HOOKING STUDY

In the fall of 2003, graduate students from Montana State University reached out to my school district looking for volunteers to participate in a pedometer study. Two questions formed the foundation of the study:

1. What is the average number of steps that a teacher takes in a typical day?
2. Do pedometers motivate people to exercise?

I was not surprised by the amount of movement that I logged during a day of teaching. In fact, I would have been disappointed had the data not shown that I was up moving and interacting with my students. For me, the personal epiphany was contained in the second question as I became enthralled with using a pedometer and monitoring my steps, mileage and caloric burn. Although I was always quite active and valued exercise, the pedometer did motivate me to literally take additional steps and bring my exercising to another level.

In a number of ways, choosing to become involved in this study has enriched my life and intensified my focus on health, wellness and personal growth. It looks like I may be "hooked" for life as I approach the fourteen year mark of step tracking. As the sophistication of the pedometers have changed, my physical goals and personal development have progressed as well. So, if you are READY for me to SET the stage to elaborate on that progression, then let's GO!

MOVEMENT MONITORING

Movement, be it physical, psychological, emotional, spiritual, relational, financial, or a host of other important components in one's life, is usually a good thing. The most basic of these, and as foundationally important as any, is physical movement. Physical movement is the most basic and perhaps easiest to monitor as well. The old "clip to the hip" pedometer has now been replaced with newer and greater technology that most people prefer to wear on their wrists. This technology is generally very enjoyable to use and connects to smart phones that track movement in steps, distance, calories, and active minutes. I love how the data is stored allowing the comparison of weeks, months and seasons. For years I had tracked my daily, monthly, and yearly step counts. Now it is even easier to look at the cumulative data to analyze patterns, set and meet goals, and to be acutely aware of my level of movement.

When I first began this lifestyle, I really didn't have an accurate concept of just how much I was or wasn't moving in a day. My tendency (as probably for most people) was to overestimate my level of activity. Monitoring my activity with a concentration on the number of steps that I take in a day, has provided an objective gauge that pushes me to reach minimum standards of physical activity while driving productivity in other areas of responsibility. For example, I know that by getting a minimum number of steps in an hour counters the dangers of sitting for too long. Reaching activity benchmarks promotes circulation, flexibility, mental alertness keeping me appropriately energized for the tasks at hand.

10K PLUS OR MINUS

The American Heart Association uses the popular metric of 10,000 steps a day as a guideline to improvement of health and wellness for the general population. This seemingly arbitrary number originated in Japan as part of a marketing campaign to sell pedometers, but the number caught on with collective support from the world-wide medical community. People attaining 10,000 steps a day have a significantly lower risk of developing heart disease, which still remains the number one killer of men and women in the United States.

Should a person really strive to reach this 10k level of activity? Isn't it true that many people are simply not capable of reaching this plateau? I would answer both questions with a simple yes, believing in the merits of the number and knowing that there are a number of factors that influence that benchmark for individuals. 10k steps in a day would indicate a healthy level of activity for the majority of people (a number that most Americans fall woefully short in attaining). Yet this 10k benchmark may not be lofty enough for some, while for others it is simply physically out of reach or unrealistic. Let's look at the latter situation and examine the sub-10k day.

Ralph Paffenbarger, the famous epidemiologist, researcher, and one of the early exercise pioneers, launched the landmark College Alumni Health Study in 1960. He studied the exercise habits of 52,000 men who had entered Harvard University or the University of Pennsylvania between 1916 and 1950. After following these men for twenty-six years, he concluded that those who exercised "vigorously" simply had a greater longevity.

Paffenbarger defined "vigorous" as jogging or walking briskly for 20 miles per week. To put that distance into context, a person who is putting in 10,000 steps a day is likely getting in excess of 35 miles per week (although the steps may be not all categorized as vigorous miles). His conclusion is not surprising to the exercise enthusiasts of the world. What I find more interesting and encouraging to people of all abilities is depicted in the following graph.

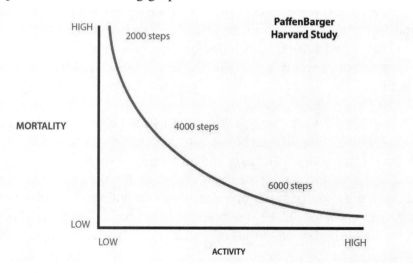

An inactive person, depicted here as getting around 2,000 steps a day, is high on the mortality axis. As one drops down the initially steep curve, the mortality rate drops at a significant rate. The first 2,000 (from 2,000 to 4,000) step increase dramatically influences the mortality rate. Moving from 4,000 to 6,000 is still a rather steep influence in reducing the mortality rate. This is great news for the sub 10k people. According to Paffenbarger graphic, 6,000 is better than simply a step in the right direction. Moving from 2000 to 6000 has an exponential benefit that is both impressive and attainable for most. Every step in fact does count, with those first four to six thousand being incredibly important.

Although the 10,000 steps in a day goal is a universally acceptable benchmark and serves as a general guideline, literally half of that figure has significant benefits and is an adequate goal for many. Again, every step really does count. Setting a goal is still a very personal decision that is subject to adjustment based on numerous considerations. Those considerations would include general positive feelings of wellness, energy level, conditioning for specific activities, weight loss, blood pressure, and the alleviation of stress. Simple movement has a cathartic effect that addresses several of the aforementioned considerations.

When I began this process, I was enamored with the goal of 10,000 steps a day. My school district had several walking programs and contests between schools. The winning school would get to house the coveted traveling shoe trophy which ended up being an honor for the committed participants. I tried to exceed the 10k mark during those contests. I felt a special accomplishment whenever I would double the mark and would star those 20k days in my exercise log. For many years I was averaging around 12,000 steps a day (yes, there were and are days that are substantially lower than the 10K mark) and feeling quite good about my activity.

But as my metabolism changed without a parallel change in my eating habits, I literally felt the need to step up my game. The 20k mark has become my personal benchmark, and for the past four years I have been averaging (not just reaching the mark occasionally) that standard. Once again, the goal is a personal one that works for me, and my plan is to continue to reach for this level of activity for as long as my body allows. I subscribe to the age old philosophy that you will "rust out before you wear out."

CONQUERING IMOGENE

Thanks to the encouragement of my good friend, Sparky Stelling, I signed up for my first trail run/walk in the fall of 2016. The Imogene Pass run covers just over 17 miles, has thousands of feet in vertical change, and takes the participants up over an elevation of 13,000 feet. The first 10 miles of the race is uphill and I found it almost impossible or certainly inefficient for me to run much of that first 10 miles. Thus, I refer to the challenge as a run/walk. My friend Mark (Sparky) had been working on me for years to join him on this race, and so I finally caved and signed up in early June. I trained quite hard during the entire summer running more than I ever had in my life, so a large proportion of my 20,000 daily steps during that time frame were of a running nature.

My thoughts were going in a multitude of directions during the week just prior to the race. I questioned if I had trained enough. I questioned if I had over-trained since I had been experiencing some knee swelling and the hints of Achilles tendinitis rearing its ugly head once again. The fear of injury coupled with a concern about not making the periodic cut off times were negative thoughts that were not serving me well. I actually began to enjoy the mental gymnastics and internal battle that was taking place, giving a big edge to the side of convincing myself that I was going to attack this challenge and perform in respectable fashion.

Years of simple step monitoring and placing such a high value on walking had given me a great foundation in getting <u>READY</u> for this excursion. I had now <u>SET</u> the challenge by taking the registration plunge and engaging in a higher level of summer training. It was time to <u>GO</u> and do this thing. I beat my goal (and now have a new one), was injury free, and was exhilarated by the experience to an almost un-describable level of elation.

BEYOND STEP MONITORING – HEALTHY REMINDERS

I have learned to use my fitness tracker for more than just a step, mileage, or calorie monitor. Every time that I look at my wrist to get a number read out, I try to use the device as a reminding apparatus. Checking my steps is also an opportunity to check in with other areas of my life. It's a reminder for me to simply smile. My pedometer becomes a gratitude-meter reminding me to acknowledge my multitude of blessings and all of the resources that I am so fortunate to have in my life. Each time I check the meter is a chance for me to take pause, focus positively and enthusiastically, and then continue with my steps – literally and figuratively.

THE HEALTH, WELLNESS, AND GROWTH JOURNEY

As the Chinese say, "The Journey of a thousand miles begins with a single step." Just get stepping. Set a step or distance goal and get going. Your goal may be 5,000 steps (very appropriate for many as previously discussed) or 2 or 3 times that amount. Set yourself up for success by choosing a goal that is somewhere between attainable and unfailing. Stephen Guise, author of the book, *Mini Habits,* set a goal of one push-up a day as a part of his new conditioning regime. He knew that he could always do at least one push-up upon getting ready, setting himself on the floor in position, and simply getting started. One push-up would always transform into dozens as his mini habit became a greater quantity habit. He applied the same type of approach to other areas of his life toward reading, and writing while on his way to becoming a successful author and self-improvement authority.

Get hooked on the GOYBASMA drug that is advocated by the esteemed wellness coordinator, health strategist, and my dear friend, Bruce Colton. The letters in that miracle drug stand for: Get Off Your Butt and Start Moving Around! Game designer Jane McGonigal found herself bedridden and suicidal after an accident. She became consumed with the science behind movement and exercise, coupled with the allure of gaming. From her research, she created the healing game that promotes resilience adding life to one's years and years to one's life. Her TED talk is entitled, The game that can give you 10 extra years of life. I highly recommend you listen to her inspirational story and unique numerical case for movement within an enjoyable game-like monitored activity.

Holistic health is founded on movement and the expenditure of energy. Movement is an unbeatable method of energy expenditure that can be meditative, therapeutic, rhythmic, positively addicting, and genuinely fun to monitor. My sincerest wishes to all of you for happy trekking and tracking!

About Joe

Joe Moriarty has been a public educator for 35 years. His experiences have included: classroom instruction as a math, science, and social studies teacher, coaching of numerous sports and extra-curricular activities, and serving as an assistant principal. His administrative responsibilities consisted of instructional leadership, student behavioral support, staff management, supervision and evaluation. He has worked with students of all ages with a special passion for middle school students.

Over the last six years, Joe has been an educational consultant with the Montana Office of Public Instruction. He is part of the Montana Behavioral Initiative which promotes positive school climate through universal expectations, common language, collection and use of data to make school-wide and individual student decisions, positive interventions, and the reinforcement of best classroom practices. Working directly with a number of schools, Joe administers fidelity checks, guides action planning, facilitates student focus groups, advocates for student voice, and conducts school assemblies in a variety of settings. He trains teachers in the MBI process, school climate and multi-tiered systems of support throughout the state of Montana.

One of Joe's greatest passions is in the area of student leadership. He has been one of the lead facilitators and presenters at MBI Youth Days for the past five years. This student conference cultivates student leadership through networking and service learning. Students are challenged to return home and continue working on developing their leadership abilities, work at enhancing the positive climate of their school, and make contributions to their community through service. Joe has also been an Adjunct Professor with the Northern Plains Transition to Teaching program at Montana State University. Within this online program, he taught non-traditional students general educational pedagogy, classroom management, and school law.

Joe is a certified speaker with the John Maxwell team whose mission is the development of leaders at all levels. Again, his experience and genuine interest with young people makes him a natural fit to be delivering the Youth Max and Youth Max Plus material to schools and youth organizations. His speaking, training, writing and coaching work is adaptable to individuals, schools and the corporate world.

In addition to his work in public education, Joe is actively engaged in the wellness arena. He recently worked as a health strategist with Two Medicine Health and Wellness and is now an owner of an emerging national company called Peak Health and Performance (PHP). The company mission includes: targeting the national obesity epidemic through coordination of medical services and nutrition, exercise, personal training, health coaching, and peak performance and character development for youth and adolescents. Joe has multiple roles within PHP from strategist and educator to personal health coach. His diverse background and holistic approach to living naturally connects his passions for wellness and education.

Joe currently lives with his wife Marcy in Bozeman, Montana. They are both public educators, active consultants, and life-long exercise enthusiasts. Marcy and Joe have raised three healthy and dynamic boys, all of whom value wellness.

You can connect with Joe at:
- email: joefmoriarty@gmail.com

For Wellness Company Information, contact:
- Peak Health and Performance
  02 Pine Valley Rd.
  Billings, MT 58101
  Tel: 406-698-5472

- Website: peakhealthus.com

CHAPTER 10

YOU ... THE THOUGHTLEADER® IN YOUR FIELD!

BY JW DICKS, ESQ.

Ten years ago, Nick Nanton and I founded The Dicks+Nanton Celebrity Branding Agency focused on the concept of Celebrity Branding You ...

How to become the Leading Exert in Your Field!

We brought to business owners and professionals, concepts like, "People Buy People" and taught how to get prospects to buy you over your competitor by getting them to know, like and trust you. The fastest, easiest way to do that was to become the expert in your field, no matter what field you were in. We taught our clients that the way to establish yourself as the expert was to write articles in your field, becoming a Best-Selling Author® on your topic, get on TV and be interviewed, and in general, provide good valuable content to your targeted customer.

This methodology of building a business based around expert status wasn't being talked about much back then, but times have changed. Today, more than ever, people want good, authoritative content from someone they recognize as the ThoughtLeader® in the field.

We launched the Agency with our book, (following our own advice on producing content), *Celebrity Branding You*, followed over the years by *StorySelling, Mission-Driven,* (all Best-Sellers) and soon our forthcoming book, *Impact.* The information in the books were supplemented by articles, websites, emails, seminars, and Facebook, and with each new media available we tried to incorporate the latest strategies in them to reach our audience.

Along the way, we attracted 3,021 clients in 33 countries, while helping clients to become Best Selling Authors®, TV Guests, make magazine guest appearances, and producing major Emmy award-winning documentaries about successful people sharing their knowledge, and non-profits changing people's lives in other ways.

As fun and exciting as these last ten years have been, the next ten years will offer us new opportunities to have a bigger impact on people's lives and their business. Many of our early teaching concepts have become mainstream. The world is moving much faster and the thirst for new ideas has moved from desire to desperation in many cases.

Information and technology have blended together and the pace today is faster. For example, while once thought a novelty, IBM's Watson is more than just a Jeopardy winner. Watson has evolved into the AI of the future in categories from medicine to financial technology, and is the platform on which IBM has rebuilt its huge, successful consulting practice.

Still, on a more foundational level, there is an even greater need for the next level expert to lead his/her field with new ideas and applications. Yes, this decade is already seeing the rise of the ThoughtLeader® – the next generation of Expert that people in every field of endeavor look for to provide a faster road for their own success.

- ❖ But what exactly is a ThoughtLeader®?
- ❖ How do you become one?
- ❖ Do you even want to be one?

These are the questions we will address while showing you the way to become a ThoughtLeader® yourself.

CONTENT MARKETING VS. THOUGHTLEADER®

In many ways, content marketing and Thought Leadership work together.

Content marketing has become a leading way to reach your prospect or customer. It is different from traditional advertising methods. Instead of brash ads yelling how good you are, content marketing is a methodology of attracting your market's attention with good solid information that your customers are seeking from a reliable source, that saves them time, money and effort required to find answers themselves.

By providing good, reliable content, people seek out the provider of this information as the Expert they could believe in to provide this information, and this creates a stronger bond of trust between the consumer and the provider of the desired content.

A ThoughtLeader® often provides original content of this type to a certain market, but he is also known for providing changing ideas, and unique insights about the direction of the topic or the field of endeavor. In many ways, the ThoughtLeader® looks beyond the surface, and "sees" new ways of using traditional ideas in a field, and may also borrow ideas from other fields adapting them to the current field they are in, or morphing into something new and different.

Elon Musk for example, is clearly a ThoughtLeader® in multiple fields. From automotive (Tesla), to solar (Solar City), to space travel (SpaceX), Musk's mind moves in and out from seemingly different worlds and he joins them in sort of a cross pollination, where the answers to the needs of Tesla may be borrowed from something learned in Solar Cities energy farms or SpaceX rocket launches.

Peter Diamandis, one of today's leading edge ThoughtLeaders® in multiple fields, was the subject of one of our documentaries entitled "Visioneer." The movie told of Peter's creation of The XPrize, a non-profit organization Peter founded to fund the answers to some of the world greatest problems. In a few short years, Peter has attracted funding for the XPrizes by leading philanthropists and major corporations offering multimillion-dollar prizes to teams of engineers and adventures racing each other competitively – to be the first to solve for the answers and win the prizes. Along the way, Peter has founded or co-founded other multimillion-dollar ventures in human longevity, asteroid mining, AI, and Singularity University, all dedicated to bold ventures for the good of mankind.

And as great as these ThoughtLeaders® are, they are only "super examples" that everyone knows, yet no more important in idea development than the young man in Orlando, Florida who created a low-priced robotic arm and 3-D printed them for a fraction of their previous cost, making them available to an entirely new and different market.

Or take 23andMe, the genetics testing company that battled the FDA for years to let them bring genetic testing to the masses for a fraction of the prices previously charged. Just recently (March 2017), they finally got FDA approval, and home-genetic test kits are on their way to a home near you. Now you can, in the comfort and convenience of your own home, find out if you have the genetic markers for certain diseases you may fear; but with this information, you are armed to look for solutions to remission or even cure.

The ThoughtLeader® today can be an Expert in any field, or as we just noted, in multiple fields. In many cases, the ThoughtLeaders® can't help themselves to provide information and ideas to others . . . "it's just what they do."

The ThoughtLeader® becomes the source of knowledge in a field and helps people sort through the content to determine truth or fiction, and to help consumers find answers to their questions from an authoritative source they are confident in and trust. Once that ThoughtLeader® status is formally or informally bestowed on someone, it is a very powerful element of trust that is hard to break up. The bond created encourages the customer to shift to the ThoughtLeaders® for other products or services provided as an exchange of value to each other.

ThoughtLeadership is also more than just providing information. It also is a smart business strategy to develop at any level of business. Just as IBM uses its computer, Watson, to grow its Cognitive Business strategy, it also uses it as a method of bringing IBM into large businesses that want information on cloud computing and data analytics. By being the Thoughtleader® in these fields through its Watson technologies, IBM is always in conversations when companies talk about them and look for someone to provide high-level services.

IBM may not always get every contract in these fields, but a company would be making a mistake not to at least consider them when looking for this type of service. "After all, a buyer would tell his board of directors

... IBM 'is' the leader in this field."

What does this business lesson teach you about using Thought Leadership as a strategic advantage in your field?

Forester's Laura Ramos says, "ThoughtLeadership impacts business at each and every stage of the buying journey, "we have found companies benefit from it in the early stage ... through more inbound inquiries and short listing for contracts, in the middle stage ... through faster sales cycles, higher close rates, and bigger deal sizes; and in the late stage ... through increased customer loyalty and higher lifetime value!"

In our own business with thousands of clients, we have seen various levels of embracement of Thought Leadership as a business strategy. Clearly, the clients who "get it" and continue to position themselves in this ThoughtLeader® role, supplying a continuing flow of authoritative content to their customer base, are rewarded by more business from their existing customer base. Additionally, the business process becomes a new marketing strategy that brings in new customers who are looking for answers from authoritative figures who freely provide answers to their questions.

This new relationship between customer and ThoughtLeader® must, like all business relationships, be continually reinforced or others will take the ThoughLeaders® place in this highly competitive marketplace.

From a strategic standpoint, the ThoughtLeader® must continue to maintain a position in the minds of their customer, through a never-ending stream of top-level information in their field. This is certainly done through email but it also must be done thorough other avenues of delivery – such as blogs, articles, newsletters, books, and videos. It is not a one-and-done strategy. It is work to maintain any relationship, and the same is true with customers who are busy with their own lives while you are popping in and out with information they want.

The difference between ThoughtLeader® strategy and hit-and-run advertising and marketing is that the strategy is long-term. Each month you follow the strategy, you are building on the previous month and your relationship with the customer is stronger. They begin to rely on you for the information they need and that begins to create a level of trust.

WHAT TYPE OF INFORMATION DO YOU PROVIDE AS A THOUGHTLEADER®?

As you might guess, this is a very important question that many people don't get.

A ThoughtLeader® provides information that their customers want:

IT'S ALL ABOUT THE CUSTOMER!

Forget that message and you are lost. I don't care how good your content is, if it isn't the type of content your customers want, they will lose interest and you will lose a customer. It is very important for you to understand this. The more you vary from the message that brought you the customer, the greater the chance you have of losing them.

If you are a financial planner and your customer was attracted to you because you talked about boomer retirement strategies, you continue to make that your message. The moment you start talking about the financial programs good for millennials, the faster you will lose the attention of the boomer. Yes, you can create a separate educational track and segment markets, but that is very difficult to do and requires double everything content-wise including another targeted web site.

Think about Dave Ramsey. Dave is known for his debt free, financial planning approach to your finances. He has talked about the same approach for years and doesn't vary his message. He continues to keep his listeners who were first attracted by this message and he gets new listeners who are attracted for the first time.

Does Dave's message get tiring sometimes? Maybe, just as we tire sometimes of a favorite song. But then when we hear it again, it awakens a sense that had paused for a moment and the good feeling comes back again. So it is in your business market and every market. The art is to try and keep the information timely but consistent, and all the great ones do it no matter what the industry. It is even true in politics, and you only have to look at Donald Trump and see the lesson applied to politics. Like him or not, the President stays on message. His buyers (his voters), never

---

[1] *The Sophisticated Marketers Guide to Thought Leadership*, LinkedIn, Jason Miller, Group Manager, Global Content and Social Media Marketing, LinkedIn Marketing Solutions

tire of what he has to say and they keep tuned in to the same message. So will your customers.

BUILDING YOUR THOUGHTLEADER® PLATFORM

To be a successful ThoughtLeader®, you must have a platform. It is your home base where you operate. Dave Ramsey's main platform is his nationally-syndicated radio show. He does have a website, books he has written and other platforms such as a Facebook page, but his main platform is his radio show. Without the radio show, he would not have the recognition that he has today.

Unfortunately, reality sets in when I tell you that at first it is very unlikely you will have a national radio show as your platform when you first start out, and neither did Dave Ramsey. In most cases, your platform will be your website as you build your reputation as a ThoughtLeader in your field.

The good news is that good, productive websites have fallen in cost the past couple of years and they tend to be less complex. All of this really depends on your budget, but if you don't have a website your business will be severely handicapped.

Your website should convey very quickly who you are, what you do, and how you can help. Remember, earlier we talked about your content being more about the customer and less about you. This is also true about your platform website. It needs to be more customer driven and less "you" driven.

This does not mean you don't have a great photo of yourself, because you must have a good one. People still react to people and a good photo with your smile is important for the guest to feel comfortable with you.

You will also share information about yourself, but the best way to do that is through testimonials of your customers. Let them brag on you and the more credibility they have, the better for you. In the beginning get testimonials from whomever you can. As your business grows and you have bigger customers, let them talk for you and the message will be received much better.

While I could go on and on about how to build your Platform Website, the best information I can give you is to go to one of my partners and my daughter Lindsay's website at: CelebritySites.com. What she forgot about websites and SEO is more than I know, and she has lots of free information that you can get and use when interviewing a Webmaster, or as a checklist if you are able to build your own.

The point about platform websites from my perspective is that a successful ThoughtLeader® must have a great platform to launch your content from and connect with your audience. Spend the time, money and effort to get it right. You will be glad you did. Please feel free to also go to our website for more content on building your business and your professional position as the expert and Thoughtleader® in your field.

About JW

JW Dicks, Esq., is a Wall Street Journal Best-Selling Author®, 2-time Emmy Award-Winning Producer, publisher, board member, and co-founder of organizations such as The National Academy of Best-Selling Authors®, and The National Association of Experts, Writers and Speakers®.

JW is the co-CEO of DNA Media, LLC and is a strategic business development consultant to both domestic and international clients. He has been quoted on business and financial topics in national media such as *USA Today, The Wall Street Journal, Newsweek, Forbes, CNBC.com,* and *Fortune Magazine Small Business.*

Considered a thought leader and curator of information, he has more than forty-three published business and legal books to his credit. JW has coauthored with legends like Jack Canfield, Brian Tracy, Tom Hopkins, Dr. Nido Qubein, Dr. Ivan Misner, Dan Kennedy, and Mari Smith. He is the Editor and co-Publisher of *ThoughtLeader®* Magazine.

JW is called the "Expert to the Experts" and has appeared on business television shows airing on ABC, NBC, CBS, and FOX affiliates around the country, and co-produces and syndicates a line of franchised business television shows such as *Success Today, Wall Street Today, Hollywood Live,* and *Profiles of Success.* He has received an Emmy® Award as Executive Producer of the film, *Mi Casa Hogar.*

JW and his wife of forty-five years, Linda, have two daughters, four granddaughters, and two Yorkies. He is a sixth-generation Floridian and splits his time between his home in Orlando and his beach house on Florida's west coast.

CHAPTER 11

THE MAGIC OF THE LITTLE PINK SPOON

BY LAURIE A. RICHARDS

Baskin-Robbins took the ice cream industry by storm in the mid 1950's and hasn't stopped selling since. Each year, 300 million people stop in for a taste, and they leave satisfied. The company's secret . . . the little pink spoon.

The iconic little pink spoon was introduced in 1953 to embrace the philosophy that customers should be able to get a taste of many ice cream flavors before purchasing. No one leaves Baskin-Robbins without a scoop of ice cream – and every customer leaves satisfied.

Baskin-Robbins makes sure of that with the little pink spoon.

Food companies and other industries have successfully embraced the give-away-samples model. We test-drive cars, try on clothes, take home little cans of paint to try on our living room walls. We read the first chapter of books, get free issues of a magazine, watch previews of movies, and get introductory weekends of premium television channels. We listen to free bits of music and even spend the weekend with our prospective new pet before signing the papers.

Why? Because we love getting a taste of something before we commit.

SHOULD YOU GIVE IT AWAY?

Retailers typically highlight three benefits to providing samples: initial sales, customer familiarity and reciprocity.

Stated simply: samples boost sales. People will make a meal of food samples offered at Costco. Some foods increase sales 2,000 percent during sampling periods. According to Interactions, a product demonstration company providing samples for Costco, in-store samples show the highest sales lifts of any in-store sales methods.

Second, sampling helps customers become familiar with products and services. Need something to take that stain out? Try this sample of a new stain remover. Wonder if you'll like our cleaning service? Let us clean your living area for free. Never used an eye cream before? Watch it make the years disappear.

The third benefit of sampling is the phenomenon of reciprocity: the theory that if someone does something for you, you'll feel a strong obligation to do something for them. For example, if you give them a taste of your new soft drink, they'll buy a six-pack. If you let them try your new aromatic lotion, they'll buy it.

Reciprocity is arguably the strongest reason sales spike during sampling. Taste a granola bar, pick up a box. Taste the wine, take home a bottle.

THE THREE MINDSETS AROUND SAMPLES

Sellers tend to be of three minds that span a spectrum of solidly against the practice of giving samples to generously for it.

Against   Strategic   For

Mindset #1:   Against Samples

The first mindset is the one that is firmly in the camp against samples. Within this mindset, you'll find several rationales to justify it.

114

"We've already invested enough… We can't afford to give it away."

"We can't get rich by giving it away…"

"If we give it away, people will think it isn't worth anything."

"Giving it away devalues it."

The most common reason new food and drink products fail is they don't get into the hands (kitchens) of consumers. How can we know that your bread is the best if we've never tasted it? And why would we spend $1 more on yours than on the tried-and-true competition?

How many inventors have hundreds—or thousands or hundreds of thousands—of widgets in their garages and storage units? These same inventors may be the ones telling that people love their product—once they use it. Instead, thousands and thousands of dollars of inventory sits…costing that inventor money for rent and space for production or other use…month…after month…after month. This happens because they couldn't get enough people to try their product and they were stuck in the mindset that samples were a bad idea.

My friend had a great idea: small scrapers made of a patented ingredient that would help clean almost any smooth flat surface (windows, floors, mirrors, windshields, counters, flat-top stoves) without scratching. I have a couple of these little gadgets around my house, and they work wonders. But, unless he gets it into consumers' hands, people will never know.

My friend laments that he can't get his special scraper into the huge retailers. Meanwhile, he has boxes of them in his basement, garage, and storage space. He's spent so much per item, he feels as though each one he gives away is an additional expenditure.

In reality, it would be cheaper to give them away than to keep them in his garage.

Mindset #2: Generously for giving out samples

On the other end of the spectrum is the overly generous "Give-until-it-hurts" mindset.

Some of my coaching friends live in this camp. Ask a question, they'll regale you with their wisdom. Give them a scenario, and they'll (loudly and proudly) share how they solved a similar problem for someone else. Instead of asking detailed questions to learn more about someone's specific situation, these folks will share their cure all   for free. (In the medical field, this would be considered malpractice!)

These same "coaches" will then cross their fingers – hopeful that they will be bombarded with phone calls from those who heard their wise words. Instead, the same people keep coming back to the proverbial feeding trough to get free tips.

Mindset #3:   Strategic Sampling

Somewhere in between the miserly "no samples" and the overly generous givers is the sweet spot of strategically sharing enough to get them wanting – and buying more. This is where you want to be. Find a smart, strategic opportunity to share your product and service knowing that some will invest and others will not.

How to design sampling for your product or service.

Designing programs to give customers a taste of what you do is easier with some products and services than it is for others. Here are five questions to consider in order to find the best way to offer a taste of your business or service:

1. **What's special about your product/service?** Not sure? Find out! That's what your sample should highlight.

   If you're an association, give them a taste of what it's like to be a member. Your organization offers events, education, resources, networking. Invite prospects to join you for an event or an educational seminar (not a meeting). Invite them to use your resources. Introduce them to someone in your chapter.

   If your service is washing cars, give customers a taste of your add-on services by offering to do an upgraded cleaning service during this visit. Once they taste how good clean feels, they'll ask for it next time.

116

For those of you selling coaching services, give them a taste of your offerings by showing them how you serve clients. Ask them questions, assess their situations. Then give them one idea (not twelve). If they like your approach, they'll be back.

For those of you with a new gadget, how can you give people a taste of what it's like to use it? At a craft fair, a woman once gave me a "taste" of her new three-inch double-stick tape. She cut off a 5-inch length, put paper on one side and removed the covering to expose the second side. Then she stuck a piece of lace on top, sprinkled it with glitter, removed the lace, and sprinkled another color of glitter for a beautiful, two-color sparkly design suitable for a card or scrapbook page. In just a few moments, she gave me a taste of her product. When I bought the roll of double-stick tape, she threw in a piece of lace so I could use it immediately. Giving me a taste of what I could do was certainly more valuable than showing me a roll of double-stick tape. The 'taste' made the sale.

2. What's your best sampling point?

A taste of bourbon chicken will get a customer to order it for lunch immediately outside of your restaurant, but what could you do to get them to ask for the frozen dinner version at the store?

My client, a friend, my sister-in-law, and I took a trip to Japan which included the climb up Mount Fuji (a story for another day). We spent two weeks in Japan in some of the most sweltering heat I've ever experienced as a tourist. In the middle of Shibuya Crossing (Tokyo's equivalent of Times Square), was a gaggle of young people handing out free hand fans emblazoned with the logo of a business that sells fans, similarly-branded umbrellas, and other goods – just steps away. For days, everywhere you looked there were fans. The right place, the right product, the right time.

3. How many do you need to sell to get a strong return?

The cost of producing and distributing samples will not be free, but the old adage holds, "You have to spend money to make money." The goal is to use samples to spur enough sales to cover your costs– and then some. How much does it cost to produce and distribute x-number of samples? How many products do you need to sell to cover cost? Is it realistic? Can you do it?

4. What other values can you leverage with samples? Look for high value/low cost opportunities.

People are looking for experiences, not just tangible goods. How can your samples provide an experience, complete with sights, smells, sounds, tastes, feelings? Will they leave the experience and tell their friends? Will they post the experience on social media?

What other values come with providing samples (outreach, goodwill, name recognition, charitable giving, etc.) How can you leverage these intangible, highly valuable features?

High value/low cost options are those that have low cost to you, but provide a high value to the customer. For example, a certificate of completion for your free coaching program may mean a great deal to someone trying to get a raise (high value). That same certificate costs you $15 for the certificate and a frame (low cost). A demonstration of your new gadget is of great value to a person who is buying something they are unfamiliar with using (high value). Your cost is in the form of your time – or the time of someone you hire and train (low cost). A free taste of your barbecue sauce ensures they buy something they like (high value), and it costs you a tablespoon of sauce out of a bottle that you'll use for more samples (low cost).

5. How do you talk about your sampling program?

If you're an association, don't ask people to come to a "meeting." People don't like "meetings." They like "events." Invite people to get a taste of your association by asking them to join you for an activity or a networking event, or to hear a featured speaker.

Provide your new atomic strength bandage to the local amusement part to hand out with paid entrance fees as an "added value" to patrons.

It doesn't have to be "free." Maybe your audience responds better to "complimentary" or "gratis." Some respond to "joining" you as your "plus one" or "guest." Still others prefer "on the house" or "without cost." If you want your audience to know your product or service is special, make sure to position your tasting experience as special. Know your audience and find a phrase that sounds valuable, worthy, and interesting.

CAREFUL: DON'T GIVE AWAY TOO MUCH

Providing a taste should be an investment – not an expense. If you give away too many tastes, you'll run out of product and go broke. Like Baskin-Robbins, you're offering tastes to help your customer find the one they like.

Give them a taste that will build demand and translate into sales. Establish a relationship, build trust, and gain credibility with your target market.

Here are three tips to avoid giving away too much:
1. Know your numbers. Track cost of samples, where they were distributed, and resulting sales. Give yourself enough time (and samples) to gather statistically relevant numbers, and make decisions based on data—not emotion. If your $1 sample results in a $10 sale, keep it up.
2. Set time and quantity limits. Encourage people to take one sample, and discourage them from taking three. (Announcing that you are "limiting" them to one makes you look stingy.) For services, tell people you'd be "happy to spend 15 minutes of your professional time." Or, you'd be "happy to answer two or three questions." When you set the limitation up front, people respect it and use the time wisely.
3. Remember your professional limitations. If you don't have the information to provide good counsel – don't. Like a physician, giving advice without good information would be irresponsible and ineffective.

Every time you put your product in the hands of a customer, there is another opportunity for a sale. *It's time to invest in some little pink spoons.*

About Laurie

Laurie Richards is a Strategic Communication Professional and President of Laurie Richards & Associates. She helps her clients become more effective communicators, better partners, more productive managers, more persuasive presenters, and more successful teammates.

Laurie believes it's not enough to be good at what you do—you have to be able to tell people about it. She has worked with thousands of executives, sales and marketing professionals, technical experts, and other leaders helping them effectively tell their stories and improve communication at every level. Known for her practical, interactive, strategic, and entertaining approach, Laurie helps clients execute outcome-based communication, upgrade customer service, improve customer satisfaction, diminish conflict, present a professional image, and improve everyday communications to directly affect the bottom line.

Laurie grew up on a farm in South Dakota where she had two terrific English and Speech teachers who taught her to always work toward effective communication and to be a lifelong learner.

Laurie began her career as a legislative correspondent for Public Broadcasting. She managed leader communications for the National Pork Producers Council—the nation's largest commodity organization and originator of the successful, "Pork. The Other White Meat©" campaign. She has hosted radio programs, managed one of the nation's fastest growing public relations agencies, launched award-winning public affairs programs, managed highly effective grassroots lobbying efforts, and facilitated professional development programs for notable clients.

Her clients span across the business spectrum – from individuals, to small business professionals, to association leaders, to Fortune 100 executives around the world. Clients describe working with Richards as "life-changing." They note her strengths as "an innate charismatic style coupled with the ability to really connect with her audience and bring practical real-life experiences we can use immediately."

Laurie has degrees in communication and business management and is working toward her PhD in Organizational Psychology. She has a variety of certifications in micro-expressions, social styles, observation, and psychological profiling.

Laurie prefers collecting experiences to collecting things. She is an award-winning international ballroom dancer, has traveled to all 50 states, has climbed Mount Fuji, and is on a mission to travel to all seven continents.

You can connect with her at:

- Laurie@LaurieRichards.com
- Twitter: @Laurie_Richards
- Facebook: https://www.facebook.com/groups/ResultsandOutcomesGroup/
- Instagram: LaurieR_Strategist

CHAPTER 12

PRACTICE

BY MOANA CAROLINE ALULI MEYER

As I approach her home, I am struck by an overwhelming sense of peace and calm. A beautiful shrine acts as an entryway. She opens the door with welcoming arms and a tremendously warm smile. Her spiky bright blue hair with hints of silver is radically youthful, yet her presence is wise, ageless. She reminds me of Hawaiian royalty, both feminine and masculine, defying labels. Acceptance, generosity, and love pour out of her entire being through her radiant, ever-playful spirit.

We sit and settle into the day, and then I am able to ask her, "If you could choose some magical gems to share with someone that encompasses what you believe to be true about life, along with what has shaped the way that you give back, what would they be?"

She pauses, beautifully contemplative. It is obvious she has so much to give that this is a ridiculous question, but then solidly, with concrete confidence she says, "practice."

He Hawai'i Au, I am Hawaiian and my name is Moana. I am not a Disney Princess. I am the ocean that holds this amazing world, and I am the middle child of seven, raised on the beautiful shores of Kailua, Oahu. I've always felt a bit different from my ohana/family, like the psychedelic sheep and there are so many variables involved. So, when you are being hurled through space-time and land somewhere in the middle of the deep blue ocean, you have to wonder! Enter my twin sister . . . in the darkness I could feel the warmth of another body and being squished. Then bam!

We came into this world one after the other – the fourth and fifth of soon-to-be seven children.

My mom lost her parents while she was young, and was the baby of six siblings, so her eldest sister raised her and had the nuns do the rest. Our mother was raised to be smart and socially acceptable . . . to be good marriage material. Women were not bred to have a mind of their own in the late '40s, but my mother did! She went off to college and continued to expand her mind. I share my mother with you to set the stage for the beauty and truth I learned so deeply from her. I have sought to emulate these gifts my entire life while feeling that greatness was outside/inside me.

My father was orphaned while young as well, and he journeyed to the islands from the Midwest in the early '50s and met my brilliant well-educated mother. He was a kind, playful-jokester-Pop and father and always told his share of very bad jokes. He loved his children.

I was a coordinated child, and at a whopping 5'2" I was a Varsity athlete in three sports: volleyball, basketball, and soccer in high school, and I went on to play these same three sports in Division One colleges. I loved sports and even though I was mostly the bench warmer and cheerleader, I loved the camaraderie and friendships I developed. I learned to persevere by staying focused, laughed a lot, and inevitably let go. And that's just to name a few!

Athletics had benefits multifold. Sports saved me. First, I learned the importance of practice from the traditional standpoint. I worked very hard to be a part of high-performing teams. The camaraderie and sense of family I felt helped heal what I felt I missed due to any shortcomings my parents may have had due to losing their own parents at such young ages.

One of my saving graces was movement and dance. We had this large orange-colored carpet in our home, it was probably a 12 x 20, in our living room. Some great old music was put on and our father loved twirling his six girls around showing us some classic moves and helping us feel the rhythm. I loved moving and even though feeling quite shy and unattractive growing up, I couldn't stop dancing. As I got older I didn't feel I was good enough to do it professionally, nor did I have the confidence to expose myself, but I kept on dancing.

I loved making stuff too. When I was ten years old, I found a wooden mechanical architectural square. I loved the shape and used it for over ten years just as a ruler. Soon I would come to know how it truly worked. With a new set of baby blue Samsonite luggage, a Timex watch and a one-way ticket to California, I headed to Pepperdine for my first two years of college. I left the Malibu coast and landed in San Diego for my final two years. After finishing university, I became a Pearl Diver in the San Diego Sea World. I looked Asian enough that even though Pearl Diving was an ancient cultural way of harvesting pearls by Japanese women, I guess being Chinese-Hawaiian was good enough. I loved pearl diving! But the tank was so cold, I ended up with an ear infection and after my first three weeks they decided to put me in the prop-making department. Everything is divinely designed!

I was finally using my creative eye and kinesthetic coordination and the square I found ten years earlier to design and build things. It was so much fun, especially as Los Angeles was creatively hopping!! I learned how to use most hand and power tools and experienced many top set-building companies as an independent designer/builder. This was more than 30 years ago when there weren't many women in the field of building and design. It was empowering to learn these skills and discover I had a natural bent for using tools and shifting spaces. I was a creative being and did not fully understand what an incredible journey I had just embarked on.

I was in my late 20's when I had my first heavy episodes of weird, undiagnosable illnesses. I wasn't eating right, resting or drinking enough water. I was young and felt invincible. I had started drinking alcohol at age 14. The '60s had passed, but the home/college parties were always happening. My environment was a full playground for addiction and I worked hard, played hard and never missed work because of it.

Enter the next 25 years of suffering from different autoimmune issues which most of the doctors could not figure out. It was a very low, frustrating time in my life and I had adopted a rulebook of nutritional lies and it was a tough hole to dig out of.

The organized religion I was raised with created its own inner toxic world. Add to the already guilt-permeating world of strict Catholicism, and the fact that I am gay, I found myself immersed in messages that did not support or validate my true essence. I was just a cute, loving kid that often got stomped on for being too friendly or loving too diversely from the familial pack.

Because the feedback loop on normalization was so, so strong and ingrained—be it nutritional habits or a sense of community at a spiritual level, I have consciously sought out many different paths of healing and expansion since my late 20's. I have come to some funny, profound, simple messages. I had to learn them the hard way, and on the brink of my sixth decade, I feel ready to rock and roll this remaining life I have! Throughout my years I found myself venturing away from Hawaii at least four times. It allowed me to learn more about myself and as I stepped into the practice of pursuing creative and alternative paths of learning and healing, I found clear, gentle ways to love myself and adopted a practice of radical self-care.

I have always felt like I was dropped into the middle of all of my ohana as comic relief. My siblings were often far more serious than me. They are all my greatest inspirations and are amazing leaders in Hawaii and Oregon. Being born a twin with an incredibly powerful sister, I always found myself practicing and embracing my own strengths. The beauty of living a bond of absolute unconditional love with someone so opposite to myself allowed me to always see situations with a constant mirror. Our differences strengthened each other and brought out our true essence.

In my mid 30's, I was recovering from a very tough bout of shingles when I came up with a really powerful concept called SmarTITAS. It was initially kind of a joke, yet the more I thought and felt about it, I began to understand what was coming through me. TITA is an endearing term back home in Hawaii meaning sister. Somewhere on the journey it was given a negative connotation of a rough, local woman; someone you don't want to mess with.

Through divine guidance, I defined TITA as a Tough, Intelligent, Tender and Artistic Sista, now Spirit. Since adopting this gift of terminology and symbolism, it has been 20 years of supporting all spirits, by teaching that we are all connected right from the start. Even though we may not feel intelligent or artistic, or if we judge ourselves for being too tough or too tender, these words have simple power and brilliance for all of us to tune in and resonate with.

I am finally feeling and understanding that I am better than I think I am. I love myself with a peaceful sense of knowing and flow with humor, and some very good swear words. Life is a liberating invigorating experience and after 30 years of struggling with very little support, a ton of guilt and shame, the old mental tape of "not good enough," I embrace and hold dear the importance of the practice of loving me for me.

As I navigated life, at an early age, I always felt ahead of my time. I wanted to express the awareness I felt. Folks back then were not awake; however, I felt joyful, jovial and awake from the get-go. I felt like everyone kept thinking I was crazy woo woo, or just too hippie. Interestingly, our culture is evolving today so rapidly; it's finally catching up with me and how I have always felt on the inside. I see the world exploding with so much MAGIC, . . . RIGHT NOW!

The desire to dwell with like-minded spirits drew me to Portland. Over the past two years, I feel increasingly happy to finally come to a town where my MOflow, Magical MOJO Poppins, can emerge into a feel-good, full-blown Mission.

I have many stories along my life path that all lead me to the same conclusion. Life is made up of many moments, all of which are a practice. A practice for compassion, Aloha Kindness and acceptance. We are already perfect just as we are. Practice does not make perfect; it's FOREVER Practicing. The practice is flowing with the many adventures and lessons we choose to create, and seeing that love, acceptance, kindness and compassion for oneself is the beauty and magnificence of each of us as one-of-a-kind. We will always be exactly as we should be. Just as we are, in each and every moment, perfect.

We are all connected in this beautiful truth and no cultural practice sums it up more effectively for me than Aloha. Aloha speaks to the essence of each of us and through shared breath. Aloha is the practice of an awakened mind. It is our Hawaiian way.

I see the world from the vantage point of three important pieces to Practice.

- One – practice loving self through lots of humor and tons of self-care.
- Two – seek to continually practice loving others for who they are and how they are, in the moment.
- Three – feel at home in your bones and practice Aloha, and acknowledge all sacred connectedness.

Ulu a'e ke welina a ke aloha!

Loving is the Practice of an Awakened mind!

I am grateful for the practice of Aloha which continues to lead the way of loving myself and then loving others. It is always a forever practicing journey. Aloha!

About Moana

Moana Carolina Aluli Meyer is the middle child of seven incredible Hawaiian artists, entrepreneurs, academics, and activists in Honolulu, HI and Oregon. She was born an artist and a goofball thrown in the middle of seven siblings as comic relief. She is also the eldest of a twin set with Dr. Manulani J. Meyer.

Moana was a Varsity Letterman athlete at Punahou High School and Division One College Varsity VB player, Pepperdine University, Malibu and an All-Star Soccer player for SDSU. She graduated from SDSU in 1982 with a BS in Recreational Management. Moana was her pledge class president for Alpha Phi at SDSU. She then returned to Los Angeles, creating and developing sets, designing and building from 1980-1990. She has transformed many private homes and businesses over a 30-year career as a space-shifting, color consulting and commissioned artist. Moana's drive to serve her community even resulted in working as an HPD officer and a counselor for runaway youth for Hale Kipa, Honolulu. She also served as a mentor for incarcerated youth transitioning from prison back into society for the CORE program.

Moana has great compassion for the betterment of all people and is the CEO – Chief Energy Officer – of her own Spirit Empowerment company called SmarTitas Ink established in 1997, up to the present (2017). SmarTitas encompasses her own line of Jewelry and Whole Hearted Playshops.

Moana had her own ART Studio and Event Space called Daspace and Studio B from 2005-2011, gathering the Arts community and offering an exciting event space for Honolulu. She is a well-respected speaker and Wellness Coach for LIV International for the past decade, and a certified HaTha Yogi. She continues to this day to offer SmarTita Personal empowerment classes and Health education. Moana is always there to lend a hand, an ear and joyful Heart!

You can reach Moana Caroline Aluli Meyer at:
- livhawaii@yahoo.com
- www.smartita.com
- mojopoppins@fb
- 808-351-4960

CHAPTER 13

COMMUNICATING YOUR BIG IDEAS: CREATING CONTENT WITH IMPACT

BY NICK NANTON, ESQ.

The bond trader was on the ropes.

He had gotten a job at a trading company in Chicago in 2008, but that position didn't last long. When the recession hit, he suddenly found himself laid off—with no prospects in sight.

But that was okay. What he really wanted to do was become a photographer. And he had what he thought was a great idea—take pictures of people all across the five boroughs of the New York City area and catalogue them by location. So, the Georgia native moved to Brooklyn. All he had was a month's worth of savings, so he moved fast and began posting pictures on his website as fast as he could take them.

. . . And no one cared.

After a year, he was surviving on cat food and taking freelance jobs to try and make ends meet. But he kept on going with his photo idea, obsessed with making it work—but he had to make one important adjustment to his approach. Instead of just spontaneously taking pictures of people around town whenever he saw an interesting image, he discovered that in New York, it was best to ask permission first—the hardened city dwellers didn't appreciate his photographic ambushes.

131

And that's when he noticed that the conversations he had to initiate to get that permission were becoming as interesting as the pictures themselves.

People for some reason would start to share intimate stories about what was going on in their lives: The parts that were hilarious, the parts that were tragic, the parts that were fascinating. He began interviewing them at length, sometimes for over a half-hour, often shocked by how much they were willing to reveal about themselves.

And that's when his "Humans of New York" project launched him into MediaMaster superstardom. Over 15 million people now follow Brandon Stanton's blog. He's had two *Humans of New York* books published and his Facebook page currently has over 18 million fans. He's been able to travel overseas to do other similar projects with people in other countries.

Best of all, he no longer has to eat cat food.

How did Stanton become a MediaMaster? Well, a while ago, Brandon Stanton accidentally tapped his phone and updated his status on Facebook. It was only the letter "Q," but within minutes it had 73 likes. Stanton, thinking that was hilarious, owned up to his mistake and posted a screenshot of the post. That post gathered more than 25,000 likes and nearly 600 comments.[1]

In our forthcoming book, *Impact*, we're going to reveal the secrets of becoming a MediaMaster, which we define as a thought leader who knows how to leverage both old and new media to build the most powerful platform possible. One of the easiest ways to do that is simply by publishing strong, consistent and unique content. The more you can generate that attracts the kinds of followers you're after, the closer you come to achieving true MediaMastery. The question for you is, which form of content best suits your persona and message—and which delivery system will create the most impact for your MediaMaster ambitions?

Let's find the answer that works for you.

---

[1] Emanuella Grinberg, "The Photographer Behind 'Humans of New York'", CNN, October 18, 2013. http://edition.cnn.com/2013/10/18/living/books-humans-of-new-york/

BLOGGING

As demonstrated by the Brandon Stanton story at the beginning of this chapter, blogging can be an incredibly effective way to create a powerful ongoing impact. And while some people believe blogging may have peaked, there is no hard evidence to back that up. As a matter of fact, the latest statistics as of this writing state the opposite:

a. 45% of marketers say blogging is their #1 most important content strategy.
b. 69% of marketers say they plan to increase their use of blogging this year.
c. Marketers who prioritize blogging are 13 times more likely to achieve a positive ROI on their efforts.[2]

That last statistic is probably key to your efforts. You may not be directly selling a product or service with your blog (and you probably shouldn't be, at least until you've established your blogging platform), but the fact that marketers are more likely to "make the sale" through the practice means you'll be able to find a receptive audience if you're able to create memorable content on a regular basis.

1. Finding Your Voice

If you're lucky, you already have a distinctive "voice" (or personality) that is unique and that people will gravitate to. If you're not that fortunate, it may take some time to develop. However, it won't develop unless you dive in and start blogging as often as you can.

That said, it may be a great idea to start writing blogs, but not actually *post* your first few blogs until you're confident in both the content and the style. Instead, look at those initial pieces as practice efforts. By spending a few weeks (or even months) honing your approach to blogging, you're making an invaluable investment in yourself. Whenever we do anything for the first time, we're bound to make mistakes. There's no reason to make those mistakes in public if you don't have to.

---

[2] Jason DeMers, "35 Content Marketing Statistics You Need to Know In 2016," Forbes.com, December 10, 2015, www.forbes.com/sites/jaysondemers/2015/12/10/35-content-marketing-statistics-you-need-to-know-in-2016/#25f7782b4363

Instead, keep writing until you feel you have a few posts worth looking at. At that point, share them with some people in your circle, hopefully people who understand your area of expertise and can react to your writing in the same way a potential new reader would, and get some feedback. If you get a consensus among your test group on how to change things up, go ahead and make the revisions based on their advice to see how you feel about the results.

There's another hidden advantage to practicing your blogging in private, by the way: You've created a potential bank of blog posts that you can access whenever you feel burnt out on blogging or just don't have the time to crank out a new post. Instead, if you find the content was basically sound in an early post, all you have to do is quickly polish it in the voice you've decided upon and post.

A voice that fits your personality will be the most natural and easiest to sustain over the long haul, allowing you to create the most long-range impact. "Write like you talk" is a common piece of advice for bloggers—and you may find it's the best way for you to get the job done.

2. The Grind

Of all the delivery systems we're discussing in this chapter, blogging can seem like the biggest grind. When you're doing it successfully, you constantly have to come up with new ideas, new content and new ways of keeping it fresh. Even writing a book is a finite proposition; blogging can go on forever (or at least seem like it!).

Seth Godin, one of the most successful bloggers of recent years (and one of the few MediaMasters who actually has his own action figure!), blogs every single day and claims to love it. In his words, "The blog is something I *get* to write—I don't *have* to write. I get to write every day and I reach over a million people. It's a really powerful tool that I would write, even if it was read by only five people."[3]

You may find you enjoy blogging as much as Godin. Or you may not! Whatever the case, here are a few tips to help you cope with the

---

[3] Dorie Clark, Stand Out, Portfolio Penguin, 2016, p. 127

never-ending task in front of you.

♦ Keep It Short When Appropriate

Some of Godin's posts are literally only a couple of sentences. Others can run to 1000 words or more. There's nothing wrong with short, punchy posts when they work. It gets you off the hook and makes for a quick read for your following. But don't make it an everyday thing. People need to hear some substance from you and that requires more than 20 words!

♦ Keep Going When Inspired

There's nothing wrong, when you have a creative wind at your back, with writing multiple posts at one sitting. By creating a pool of posts that you can use whenever, you give yourself the freedom to take the day off from blogging when you need to. You can even create a whole week's worth in one writing session if you're prolific enough.

♦ Break into Parts When Necessary

Tackling a topic that requires some lengthy explanations? Don't short-change the subject matter by trying to cram it into one single blog. Instead, first take as much space as you need to write up the whole post, then go break it into parts. Creating a series of blogs on a subject people are interested in has two advantages: (1) It enables you to create a set of blogs in advance and (2) it motivates a casual reader to come back the next day (and begin to hopefully make checking out your blogs a habit!).

♦ Write about Stuff You WANT to Write About

When you're passionate about what you're doing, you get more excited about doing it. So, make that idea work for your blog. Tap into your enthusiasms when you're writing your blog (as long as they're relevant to your area of expertise)—and feel free to occasionally write about fun aspects of your life. For example, if you have a dog or cat…well, people love pets (you may have noticed one or two animal videos on Facebook), so write about some cute thing yours did. Bonding with your readers isn't just about your profession—it's also about who you are as a person. The more you can share about yourself personally, the more people will be interested in you.

3. Your Blogging Platform

In general, you'll want to set up your own blogging site, either as an add-on to your current website or by setting up a dedicated page through a provider such as WordPress, which allows you to choose your own specific visual theme, monitor comments from readers and so forth.

Wherever you blog, you want to make sure that you're able to immediately share any posts on your various social media accounts, because that's where you'll obviously attract the most eyeballs. Twitter, Facebook, and LinkedIn, for now, are most likely the most important sites to utilize to spread the word—and you may want to hit those sites (especially Twitter) two or three times a day to make sure your message isn't getting lost in the shuffle.

And, by the way, if you want to know a great way to avoid your blogs getting lost in the shuffle, always try to use an arresting visual (photo or graphic) for each blog you write. Content with relevant images gets 94% more views than content without relevant images.[4]

VIDEO

And speaking of images, video content contains a multitude of them—which is why it continues to explode in popularity for content providers. There's no question that text content dominated the online world through the early years. Back then, few people had the internet speed to download or play videos efficiently—and the technology wasn't yet in place to easily create or post them.

In 2005, YouTube made its internet debut, bandwidth grew and suddenly video experienced explosive growth. That growth continues today, because, according to a recent study by Usurv, consumers are 39 percent more likely to share content if it's delivered through video, and 36 percent more likely to comment and 56 percent more likely to give that video a "like." And according to a Nielsen study, 64 percent of marketers expect video to dominate their strategies in the near future. Finally, Facebook claimed in 2016 that there were more than eight billion video views and more than 100 million hours of video being watched on the platform daily.

---

[4] Jesse Mawhinney, "37 Visual Content Marketing Statistics You Should Know in 2016," http://blog.hubspot.com/marketing/visual-content-marketing-strategy#sm.0001rjktb08die2myfy1ici yjxc4l

And that's why we've seen in recent years the rise of YouTube "stars," people with names like Yuya and Fernanfloo, who make millions of dollars off the massive amount of hits their videos get. Now most of you out there may not have any idea of who these online celebs are, but hordes of internet users do. Most of what they do appeals to users under 30 as they show viewers how to apply makeup, demonstrate the latest fashions, share the latest video game tips and the like.

What do all of the above activities have in common? They're very visual—and can't really be described properly with the written word. That means if your expertise involves something along those lines, something that screams to be demonstrated visually, video blogging, or "vlogging," might be the right way to go for you.

- **Is Video Right for You?**
  To make videos that will have impact, there needs to be a strong performance element in place. But...if you feel uncomfortable performing for the camera, and it shows, you'll either want to keep practicing until you smooth out those wrinkles or stick to text-based blogs. Obviously, you don't want to put out an inferior product that will drive away viewers rather than attract them. It is worth putting in the effort to practice until you are able to finally relax and be natural on camera—that kind of ability will translate well to other MediaMaster opportunities. We've been doing videos for years, so they're kind of second nature for us—we don't have to sweat going into our studio and talking about whatever message we want to put out there. The only way to get to that place is to keep doing videos—even if the only person who sees the results is you—while you're still developing your video personality.
- **Video Tips**
  Much of the advice we offered for blogging also applies here. You can make videos of varying lengths, you can shoot a bunch in a row to be more efficient and you can do a series of videos about a single topic when you have enough material. But there are a few additional tips that only apply to video:
  - ◆ **Give It Some Visual Value**
    Too many people simply shoot themselves against a blank wall or, worse yet, use webcams to make low quality videos featuring their distorted heads against a background of a messy office or living room. Instead, create an attractive space where

you can maintain a consistent and eye-pleasing look. It doesn't have to be anything elaborate—but it doesn't have to resemble a hostage video either!

♦ **Make Yourself Comfortable (and Look Good)**

Do you deliver your message better sitting or standing? Do you feel better in casual clothes or "professional attire?" Is your delivery better if you speak off-the-cuff about a topic or if you memorize a series of points? The more videos you make, the more you'll see what works better for you—and your audience. It's a tricky balance, but your performance should be the priority. Make sure your set-up makes you feel at ease and enables you to communicate in the most intimate person-to-person manner.

♦ **Maybe Don't Use "Take One" – Unless…**

The beauty of video is, unlike many things in life, you can do it over until it's right. There's not much sense in putting up a video that could easily be a lot better if you were just willing to do it one more time. Having said that, some of our clients have made some very memorable videos by keeping in some giant thing that went wrong in the middle of it and even making fun of it. People always love "bloopers"—as long as it's a mistake that doesn't harm your brand in any way.

♦ **Add Other Production Elements**

This requires a bit of extra editing time, but adding the right music, extra graphics, etc., can really make a video shine. You most likely don't want to take on too much post production if you're trying to put out a few videos a week, but think about at least adding a piece of music under your videos and branding them with an open and close that features your name, perhaps a consistent title for your series and your website address.

VIDEO VS. TEXT

According to a recent article in *Psychology Today*[5], reading blogs and watching videos require two different brain processes. Watching a video is very passive. It's much less demanding and more of an automatic process, asking a lot less energy and effort of us. Reading, in contrast,

---

[5] Liraz Margalit, "Video vs Text: The Brain Perspective," Psychology Today, May 1, 2015, https://www.psychologytoday.com/blog/behind-online-behavior/201505/video-vs-text-the-brain-perspective

is much harder on our heads; we need longer attention spans and deeper cognitive efforts to get the job done.

So that's a win for video, right? Well, not so fast. Because reading requires so much more focus on our parts, it also means our minds are much more active when we do it. That means the reader will absorb and take in the content at a much deeper level. Also, written content can be a little more sophisticated and comprehensive—as well as give the reader the opportunity to cut and paste for their own usage.

Text-based content has also been shown to be more critical to actual decision-making. When people have to make a choice, they want to be able to read the pros and cons before committing. That's why sales letters are still important to marketers.

Here are a few questions to ask yourself when deciding on which way to go with your blogging efforts:

Video: Do you need the visual punch that video brings you? Are your performance skills high enough that video just makes sense for you? And, frankly, would you rather simply blab into a camera than have to sit down and sweat over what should come out as a professional piece of writing?

Text: Are you more comfortable writing than being on camera when it comes to sharing content? Are your writing skills one of your strong suits? Does your content require a great deal of concentration and thought from your audience? Are you building an ongoing narrative that will be more effective in print rather than on video?

Your personal Video vs. Text call may be a little difficult to make—if so, try doing a few blogs each way and see which medium works best for you. Get input from trusted friends and see if you can get a consensus if you're still unsure.

And don't forget, as Brandon Stanton proved, mixed media blogging can also be incredibly successful.

<u>WRITING A BOOK</u>
Writing a book used to be the fastest path to MediaMaster superstardom.

By laying out a new and comprehensive philosophy, manifesto or "how-to" that resonates with the public, authors instantly created a platform for themselves that propelled them into the limelight. Media interviews, speaking tours and, of course, even more books, enabled them to become celebrities in their own right and build their MediaMastery into fulfilling and lucrative careers.

And all of that is still true today.

As a matter of fact, it may be even more true today, because publishing has become so much easier and more affordable. Putting our clients into books is one of our favorite ways to bring them prestige and prominence in their professions or marketing niches, because becoming an author is still ... well, in the words of Ron Burgundy from *Anchorman*, "kind of a big deal." And becoming a *Best-Selling author*, a status which our marketing systems allow our clients to achieve, is a really, really big deal! You are perceived as an expert at a whole different level if you've got a book to your credit—and that gives an incredible boost to people's perception of you. Many people (including us!) have closed some impressive deals based on their authoring success.

To truly be a MediaMaster in any age, it's almost essential at some point to put out your own book.

- **When to Publish**

    Most publishers won't even consider a book unless the author already has a robust online presence in place. They want a pre-built audience that's ready to snap up what you have to say (and they have to sell).

    Self-publishing is also a great approach for many. Once you've put in some time blogging and hopefully building a following, you will have a dedicated group primed and ready to buy your book. Not only that, you will have had some time to really hone your message and content, to see what grabs your audience and what leaves them cold. Through this process, you'll be able to create a book with true Impact. And, if you're lucky, you can even repurpose some of your blogging content and make it a part of your book, facilitating the actual writing experience.

    Of course, if you feel like you already have the perfect book inside you, you may want to reverse the process and put out your book as quickly as possible to establish yourself. This will give you immediate credibility in your field and a platform to build from. In this case, you will probably have no choice but to self-publish, but, again, there are an incredible number of advantages to having the book available to help promote yourself and your ideas. And this time you can repurpose content from the book for blogs, articles, speeches, etc.

Remember, you don't have to actually write the book yourself. A talented ghostwriter can help you work out a chapter structure and then interview you to draw out the content you want in the book. From there, they'll be able to capture your voice and create a polished, finished manuscript.

BOOKS, VIDEO & BLOGS

Books, video and blogs are three important ways we advocate for delivering content to your current and potential followers, clients and customers. There are others that can come into play—various informational products, speeches, podcasts, etc.—if you're inclined to explore them. Most of them work off the same principles we've discussed in this chapter.

What's important is to discover which delivery system best suits you personally and also allows you to reach a big enough audience. When you discover the right balance, that's when you will really make a huge impact.

About Nick

An Emmy Award-Winning Director and Producer, Nick Nanton, Esq., produces media and branded content for top thought leaders and media personalities around the world. Recognized as a leading expert on branding and storytelling, Nick has authored more than two dozen Best-Selling books (including The Wall Street Journal Best-Seller, *StorySelling*™) and produced and directed more than 40 documentaries, earning 5 Emmy Awards and 14 nominations. Nick speaks to audiences internationally on the topics of branding, entertainment, media, business and storytelling at major universities and events.

As the CEO of DNA Media, Nick oversees a portfolio of companies including: The Dicks + Nanton Agency (an international agency with more than 3,000 clients in 36 countries), Dicks + Nanton Productions, Ambitious.com, CelebrityPress, DNA Films®, DNA Pulse, and DNA Capital Ventures. Nick is an award-winning director, producer and songwriter who has worked on everything from large-scale events to television shows with the likes of Steve Forbes, Ivanka Trump, Sir Richard Branson, Rudy Ruettiger (inspiration for the Hollywood blockbuster, *RUDY*), Jack Canfield (*The Secret*, creator of the *Chicken Soup for the Soul* Series), Brian Tracy, Michael E. Gerber, Tom Hopkins, Dan Kennedy and many more.

Nick has been seen in *USA Today, The Wall Street Journal, Newsweek, BusinessWeek, Inc. Magazine, The New York Times, Entrepreneur® Magazine, Forbes,* and *FastCompany.* He has appeared on ABC, NBC, CBS, and FOX television affiliates across the country as well as on CNN, FOX News, CNBC, and MSNBC from coast to coast.

Nick is a member of the Florida Bar, a voting member of The National Academy of Recording Arts & Sciences (Home to the GRAMMYs), a member of The National Academy of Television Arts & Sciences (Home to the EMMYs), Co-founder of The National Academy of Best-Selling Authors®, and serves on the Innovation Board of the XPRIZE Foundation, a non-profit organization dedicated to bringing about "radical breakthroughs for the benefit of humanity" through incentivized competition – best known for its Ansari XPRIZE which incentivized the first private space flight and was the catalyst for Richard Branson's Virgin Galactic.

Nick also enjoys serving as an Elder at Orangewood Church, working with Young Life, Downtown Credo Orlando, Entrepreneurs International and rooting for the Florida Gators with his wife Kristina and their three children, Brock, Bowen and Addison.

Learn more at:
- www.NickNanton.com
- www.CelebrityBrandingAgency.com

CHAPTER 14

"TELL ME HOW YOU WANT TO LIVE!"

BY TORSTEN MAU

"In life, you'll always be faced with exactly the situation you're currently able to solve!" he said on the phone. One of the most successful entrepreneurs I know told me this in a memorable phone call in 1991. "So, everything's always taken care of," he added.

This phone call triggered the most incredible turning point I've ever experienced in my life.

I was born in 1966 in East Germany – so, behind the Iron Curtain. My father left our small family when I was barely a year old. We moved to another city and my mother met another man and they eventually got married. This man adopted me and my sister, and he became the best father I could ever imagine. It was the beginning of a wonderful time. He taught me how to ride a bike and harvest honey in our own bee hut. It really was a fabulous time. But then, when I was just nine years old, my father killed himself in our apartment. My sister found him.

Now restless times began. My mother met a different man a year later and we moved to his place in another village. It was a true idyll, a small village right by the lake. But then my stepfather raped my sister and often tried to abuse me sexually. I was 10 years old at the time, and my mother escaped with me and my sister to another city and we started all over again.

We then moved twice to a different place before my mother met yet another man, and we moved again into his house in a new city. I was now just 16 years old and beginning an apprenticeship as a heating engineer. But my new stepfather quickly turned out to be a highly aggressive and oafish brute. He tried to knock me around on several occasions, but fortunately I was faster and could flee the house every time. But then one Friday evening when I came home from campus, my key no longer fit in the front door. The locks had been replaced, inside the lights were on, but no-one opened the door. When the lights in the bedroom went out just before midnight, I finally realized that I was stuck outside. They had thrown me out at 16.

A period of homelessness began. Sometimes I slept at friends' places, for a short time with my sister, and later in dorms. In spite of this, I successfully completed my apprenticeship as a heating engineer.

I got my own apartment when I was 18. One day, there was a very timid knock on the door. I opened it and my mother was standing there. She stood there looking very ashamed, with only one small bag. She was broken down by violence and at the end of her rope. After kicking me out, her husband had brutally beaten her, landing her in hospital multiple times, and degraded her in every imaginable way. Finally, she had escaped to a women's shelter, was now homeless, and had managed to make it to me. I took her in, took care of her, and six months later she was back on her feet.

I myself was now 20 and wanted to get out of the totalitarian regime of East Germany and into the world. I submitted a request for a departure from East Germany to the government authorities. A year of dull and underhanded interrogation began at the intelligence service. Always very close to prison. Then the secret service people began to harass my mother all the time and finally issued her with a country-wide ban on working as an engineer. So, I withdrew the request for departing East Germany. The price for my mother was too high.

When the Wall suddenly fell in 1989, I founded my first company a short time afterwards, but I went bankrupt a year later. I had no money left, the loans were cancelled by the bank, and the bailiff came for me.

Sometime later, my mother suddenly disappeared overnight along with all her furniture from her apartment, and to this day is still nowhere to be found. The exact same thing happened with my sister, and she too has completely vanished.

Back in 1991, I no longer had the strength to go on. I was at the end of my rope. I was 24, completely bankrupt, full of anxiety, and had not a shred of optimism left. But I knew this incredibly successful entrepreneur. And in my time of need, I called him. Maybe he'll even give me money, I thought.

Instead, he gave me this sentence: "In life, you'll always be faced with exactly the situation you're currently able to solve!"

He said a few other things, but this sentence was the greatest gift anyone had so far ever given me. This sentence completely changed my life. I began to change my thinking bit by bit to be in line with the direction and meaning of this sentence, and everything else, my whole life, changed with it.

Today, in 2017, I am a very successful entrepreneur, international author, father, head of sales, international speaker, and empowerment expert. I travel around the world, speak to many people, and experience the incredible privilege of supporting and helping other people with my knowledge and experience on their journey to a fabulous life.

I am sharing my story with you, because I know that we humans load ourselves not with our actual experiences, but with our innate evaluation of these experiences. They make up our world view, our paradigm. Our basic attitude is guided by them. And that drives our way of thinking.

You know, many people think they can't do anything. Some even think they were given an exceptionally bad lot. Or they think it wouldn't matter if they changed something. In truth, these people think they themselves are not important enough. And that it has no influence on the lives of others. This is simply not the case. Every life is important. Every human being – including you!

Today I'm opening my Holy Grail for you here, I'm opening my safe for you and showing you my biggest personal methods to a successful life. They are the parameters that establish your basic attitude towards ways of thinking and behavior. It is on the basis of these that the events that form a fantastic and fulfilling life are put together.

PRINCIPLE NO. 1:

Immediately delete the word "guilt" from your vocabulary and replace it with "responsibility"!

It's very easy to point your finger at others and loudly say: you're to blame! But in truth, any unresolved situation with an undesirable outcome demands a different answer until the situation or the problem is solved. If you blame others, you reject the part of the responsibility and learning experience that is yours in this matter. You are involved in the matter, or you would not blame someone else. It is imperative that you take responsibility for your part in the matter. Only then have you accepted the lesson of the situation and your life muscles can grow. If a situation like this happens again in life, your experience has trained you and you can easily clear the hurdle.

Note: *responsibility makes you strong!*

PRINCIPLE NO. 2:

First comes the decision, then the way reveals itself - never vice versa!

We can't test-drive our lives. We have to live and we have to bear and live out the consequences of our decisions. That alone puts us on the right track and allows us to grow. That's why it's necessary to reconcile the two decision-making centers inside us, namely our heart and our brain. The brain needs data and facts to make a decision. If it doesn't have any, it rejects it. When the heart makes a decision, it speaks with the language of feeling and intuition, but then has no data or facts to carry it out. This means many of our heart's desires often remain unfulfilled. So, we should make sure we combine the two decision-making centers inside us. The heart and gut feelings guide the way, and the brain must implement decisions with its reason and planning tools.

Note: *Your decisions are the precursors to what you will later hold in your hands!*

PRINCIPLE NO. 3:

You can't win a downhill race on a ski slope with diving equipment!

Your path must lead into a world in which you want to live! It's essential to know where that is and where you belong. This is not optional! It's an obligatory matter and there is absolutely no alternative for anyone in our Western world! You need to find out whether you were given diving equipment in life or ski equipment. It makes little sense to slide around in the snow with flippers for the 85 years of your life. This will definitely end in a great deal of frustration. It means that you can't be a role model later on for your children, friends, and partners. Lost in this way, you can't pass on things that work. And so, the great idea of evolution passes you by: Pass on what works! So, get back on your feet, look in the mirror and into your heart and then tell yourself without a hint of self-consciousness who you are and what is indispensable to you personally in your life. And then find the ideal way to live with your equipment.

__Note:__ It is not noble to cultivate false ways of living and thinking until a change doesn't seem to be worthwhile anymore. This is denial! Instead, be brave!

PRINCIPLE NO. 4:

Sometimes you have to go back a few steps to take a run for the big leap!

If things sometimes fail or do not go according to plan, never be too hard on yourself. Resistance only serves to illustrate the areas in which you currently need to learn and grow. If the obstacles become bigger, you are getting closer to your goal and your need to learn will become correspondingly larger. This will require your full attention and your time. And this time is sometimes missing in other places. That's why we can't always carry out our plans on time. We simply didn't consider the complexity of the matter. When life prompts us to grow, it presents us with many challenges. It might take two months instead of a week. But if you overcome this postponement with a positive outcome, you're definitely on the next level.

__Note:__ If you have to avoid a few cliffs, but then return to the planned course, you will still reach the destination port – a little later perhaps – but now with the experience of cliffs. YES!

PRINCIPLE NO. 5:

Never make your vision of tomorrow dependent on yesterday's results!

Every hot air balloon can fly again. Yesterday's weather does not determine how you start today. If you make decisions today based on yesterday's weather, this can have fatal consequences. The conditions are probably quite different today. Do you want to go to Hawaii but a look in your wallet banishes the thought? This proves nothing! It only shows that you cannot fly today. But you can make a plan by setting out what activities you need to do and when, if you want to be in Honolulu in six months' time. This applies to a trip, a job change, as well as to founding your own company.

Note: Always look objectively into your heart when you visualize the future of your life. The results of yesterday are in your thoughts anyway, because they determine your point of view, where you stand now, today!

PRINCIPLE NO. 6:

You bear responsibility, even if it goes wrong!

You can't consign your garbage to your life. Neither the physical nor the mental garbage. Think about how it starts with the receipt left behind in the supermarket trolley, with the secretly-discarded car tires in the nature reserve, or the public toilet left in a terrible state, and it ends right in the middle of your quality of life. What you give to others is you sowing your next harvest. Everyone cultivates their own lives. What grows on yours is what you sow. And life is just: no one can ultimately refuse their own harvest. If you go bankrupt, it's not all over. Sweep up the shards, clean everything thoroughly, and leave behind a decent playing field for those who come after. This is the only way to start again with neutralized chances.

Note: Integrity is essential for an exceptionally-fulfilling life. The wrong friends and ideas fall away automatically from those who have integrity. Integrity purifies!

I remain yours with the very best wishes for a completely brilliant and fulfilled life.

Cordially yours,
Torsten Mau

About Torsten

Torsten Mau helps his customers and clients in a very effective way to achieve the status of a largely self-determined and successful life. Inspired and driven by his own challenging life story, after his training as a heating engineer he had a strong desire to pave the way for himself and others to a fulfilling, self-determined life.

When after some time, he switched from construction site assembly to sales, in addition to his job as an external salesman, he traveled time and time again over the years to see interesting contemporaries with his purpose in mind. He interviewed them about issues regarding their life success and their views on the most important questions for a fulfilling and self-determined life. In this way, a highly valuable, and above all unique collection of methods, views and authentic recipes emerged. He then carefully evaluated and brought them together piece by piece, and combined them with his own experiences.

And although he had only a normal school-leaving certificate and thus had neither his high school diploma nor a university education, he was very successful in the application of his knowledge, and ultimately realized his own dream of a largely self-determined and successful life. And of course, he continues to conduct his interviews.

Torsten Mau writes books and essays as an international author, works as the head of sales in a company with 400 employees in Germany, and additionally, is the Founder and CEO of his own company, TORSTEN MAU – SPECIALIST for PERSONALITY DEVELOPMENT – in which he shares the methods, recipes, and insights for a truly fulfilling and self-determined life with as many people as possible. He is also a recognized speaker and empowerment expert and speaks on the international stage. In 2017, for example, he spoke on the German TV station "Hamburg1" and at the United Nations Headquarters in New York.

You can contact Torsten Mau at:
- www.TorstenMau.com

CHAPTER 15

THE YOGA OF SUCCESS
—BALANCING BODY, MIND AND SPIRIT FOR PROSPERITY, ACHIEVEMENT AND ABUNDANCE

BY SRADDHA PRATIVADI, MD

As we grow more technologically driven and enamored with the latest gadgets, the data shows that we are far from achieving our nation's physical and mental health goals. As a physician, I daily hear about the increasing stress and declining happiness that is being achieved in the United States. Much of my effort in the office is put into reorienting people to the roots of health. In fact, I would argue that getting back to the foundations of wholeness and living a purposeful life is critical to this dialogue. It is also critical to achieving business and institutional goals. Taking time to honor your body, cultivating the faculties of the mind to serve as a catalyst for achievement, and self-reflecting to connect your spirit to the large reality of the Universe and your higher purpose, are all needed to power the individual and collective positive potential.

This important topic is gaining more recognition across communities and institutions. Very few, however, truly understand what health, wellness and prosperity truly mean at each of these levels. Understanding each level – body, mind and spirit and the deep interconnectedness of these different aspects of our human experience can empower individuals and institutions alike to tap into their most powerful asset: human potential.

There is a common thread between body, mind and spirit – it is energy. It is universal intelligence. It is consciousness. When you understand this, you understand your own power and your own potential. You will understand how to catalyze success in your organization.

My name, Sraddha, comes from the Sanskrit root, H'rd, which means Heart. Sraddha means single-minded faith, devotion, concentration and attention, usually in attainment of an intellectual or spiritual goal. I think it's interesting that the oldest language on the planet gets meaning from the heart for aspects of the intellect and spirit. But let's explore this more through the lens of achieving your individual, business or institutional potential.

The quadruple aim of healthcare can be translated into any business as achieving high standards in customer experience, achieving results and outcomes with your products and services, reducing costs, and the well-being of the team. This was seen regularly by many old American corporations with a social priority – these institutions understood that the well-being of the corporation was a reflection of the well-being of the individual people, in fact it was one of their goals – not just money.

By implementing principles of health for the body, mind and spirit, any community or organization can tap into its potential and achieve its goals.

In a system that strips individuals of so much of their power – including their own power to heal themselves and to think for themselves – I believe it is imperative to rediscover our own capacity to heal and create a culture in which this is possible for everyone. To do this we must first have an awareness of who we are and the gifts we have within our reach.

There is a lot of talk about body, mind and spirit. These are popular terms nowadays, but I feel we are not investing the effort to really understand these things meaningfully as they relate to our humanity. By understanding how these three connect together and how to bring out the best of these three aspects of everyone in your family or organization, new heights and visions can be reached.

The ancients recognized that even though we are spiritual beings having a human experience, attention to the body is fundamental to the path of the mind, intellect and spirit.

The 8-step process described in Ashtanga Yoga from the Vedic culture of India starts with behavior choices, then a taming of the body. This prepares the mind for higher levels of concentration and function. With a tame and controlled mind, one can reach their infinite potential by connecting with spirit.

The entire first half of the path of yoga is actually having to do with physical actions and the body in daily life. So, when most of us think of the body, we may think of these things – molecules, bones, muscles, DNA, blood, birth, disease, death. Medical students study detailed diagrams explaining the physical structures of the body. We know there are concrete things we can do to sustain the body and maximize its health.

In our stressful professions, something easy like alternative nostril breathing is so easy to do to coordinate the hemispheres of our brain, create heart coherence by going from a place of fear, frustration and anxiety to one of gratitude and flow. These processes are important because they create a harmony in the body.

Coherence is a measure of the pattern in the heart's rhythm, which is independent of the amount of heart rate variability, and reflects an orderly and harmonious synchronization among various systems in the body such as the heart, respiratory system and blood pressure systems. In yoga, this is called Nadi Shodhana and is part of pranayama or the science of breathing.

Artists like Alex Grey render different images to challenge us to think about the body differently. Are we only mass? Is our body only mass? Is there more?

We know babies, even if fed physically, will die if they are not loved and touched. How can this be possible? Aren't we just our bodies? Are we hurting patients by just looking at the body and not actively engaging with their mind and spirit?

The HeartMath Institute is studying some of the mysteries of the human heart and have shown that the heart has an immense electromagnetic field far more powerful than the brain, shedding light on the fact that the heart is much more than a beating muscle pumping blood through our vessels. It has its own immense energy field. There are high-thinking people who are looking at this dynamic and putting modern language to it.

There is an emerging field of science with some of the most reputable people of our time involved – biofield science. A recent acquaintance of mine, Dr. Shamini Jain, is the founder and director of the Consciousness and Healing Initiative based in San Diego. Her team writes here . . . "A key ingredient in the recipe for advancing the evolution of human health is self-empowerment, which can only emerge with clear recognition of one's own capacity for healing. Examples from clinical and research areas such as mind-body medicine, placebo, psychoneuroimmunology, and neuroscience remind us that our capacity to activate our own internal healing response is within our human capabilities."

Your body and its care are critical to your mind and spirit. I had a patient who had an endometrial cancer scare. After her surgery, she and I spoke about next steps in her health. I found out she is a religious Christian woman with a prominent role in her church. I learned more about her faith-life and that she actually saw attention to her physical health as contrary to her faith and spiritual path. I asked her what her purpose is. She said to do God's work. I asked her if she could do God's work in helping others if she were sick all the time due to her lack of attention to the instrument of work given to her. The lights turned on. She proceeded to make immense changes in her lifestyle and health in the coming year. We had shifted her paradigm. In which part of us do these paradigms live and function? In our mind. Paradigms rule the mind.

Understanding paradigms is critical to guiding change in a patient, client, family or organization. Knowing how to be the master of your own mind is critical to being an effective healer or leader. Faculties of the mind include Memory (knowledge), Will (Focusing and magnifying power), Perception (Lenses), Reason (Paradigms), Intuition (Connection to infinite wisdom), and Imagination (Connection to infinite possibility). The mind is the functional aspect of you dealing with thoughts and emotions. Understanding the mind will help you be the healthiest leader, businessperson, family member you can be, and also be of highest positive impact to those around you.

There are many forms of meditation, but those codified in the 8-limb yoga path are in an effective sequence to help you achieve results – the first phase of mind conditioning is withdrawing from input from the sense organs – Pratyahara. Next, bringing in awareness to your inner self and your emotions is necessary. This is Dhyana or more of a mindfulness meditation. The next step is Dharana, or more of a transcendental meditation, shown in scientific studies to be the more powerful of the two in creating real biological, spiritual and mental changes in people.

Because you are not just your physical body, you are constantly impacting others through the non-physical parts of you. Albert Einstein told us that everything is energy (through his famous equation), bringing an ancient truth into a language modern people all over the world could relate to. Why should you pay attention to this? Because knowledge of $E = mc^2$ has been used to create massive death and destruction on the planet, but it has also been used to create massive opportunities for growth and good work. Just as physicists can manipulate the energy of atom-splitting, as healers, businesspeople and family members, we must understand how to alter our own energies to create the best outcome while we are rendering our services and going about our duties. We use meditation to maximize our intellectual and emotional self-control and ignite the mental faculties of imagination and intuition.

Many say these are the aspects of the mind closest to spirit because they require that we connect ourselves to the fields of consciousness and infinite intelligence of the Universe – the place where "anything is possible."

Physicists talk about this beautiful concept called the Zero Point field. Everything must follow the laws of the Universe. Everything is transformation and transmutation of energy. One form of energy turning into another form of energy. Zero point field, atoms, gravitational fields, consciousness, thoughts, sound-transmutation of energy is the common thread. I love the biblical saying, "And first there was the harmonic resonance," incorrectly translated into English as "the word" from Jesus's Aramaic. This also demonstrates an understanding of a fundamental truth of the Universe. We can use this knowledge in everyday life – from relationships to achieving wealth.

I use yoga because it is an ancient practice from India that has unquestionably been established as valuable to the Western healing experience. Some magic starts to happen when you progress past the meditation phase to connect to the divine, zero point field or the supreme intelligence, whatever word is consistent with your beliefs. Additionally, transcending thinking beyond death requires one to connect to the larger reality of the Universe while remaining connected and grounded to your purpose on the planet. Yogic science recognized this along the many paths - Leadership (Raja yoga), Service (Karma Yoga), Faith (Bhakthi Yoga) or Discipline (Hatha Yoga). There is a path of exploration for everyone.

But can we elevate this conversation and structure it in such a way it is applicable in our work, whether it be healing or business? Can we engage in this conversation in a more sophisticated way than just saying, "I go to yoga class and have an acupuncturist" as a healing professional or everyday citizen? As a business person, can we systematically implement this knowledge into our organization to catapult financial and intellectual achievements? Yes, yes and yes. Studies have been done showing how incorporating a body, mind and spirit approach to support employees and staff to reduce injuries, elevate morale and improve patient outcomes by directly taking care of those who work face-to-face with customers, patients and clients.

We have had an evolution of language but we need more than medicine or some flaky approach to body, mind and spirit health. We need healing. We need a radical change in the language of business – money as a goal is a dumbed-down objective of a business. You need to think bigger, deeper and more holistically to create success with the evolving consciousness of humanity.

The main point here is that healing is a communal process. This requires a healing culture, a complete set of paradigms of thinking that place health as the first wealth.

We are social creatures and are healthier together. All organizations need to design their workflows and organizational cultures to honor this basic aspect of being human. A healthy community is a prosperous community. A healthy employee is a productive employee.

I want us all to become richer in Text Health in all its forms. Through

RicherTogether.org we are working to change this dialogue. Through Positive Power Ups, subscribed to at DoctorP3.com, we are working to inspire individuals toward their higher potential through a process I call the Seventh Lotus Process. Here is a simple description of this powerful process:

Connect with your heart – what makes your heart sing?

From here, create a vision of the physical manifestation of this feeling. What does your image look like? . . . a relationship? . . . a certain dollar number of your bottom line? . . . an academic achievement?

What does this image feel like? What emotions are you feeling? Are they positive or negative? Aim for emotions closer to love, gratitude growth and expansion.

- ❖ What guidance are you getting for steps to take to achieve it? Take the first step. As you do, the next step is revealed to you.
- ❖ What guiding principles do you live your life by? Do your actions and vision represent these principles?

Write down the visions that come to you and start to take action toward them!

So we see how when we are connected to spirit, we know who we are, what our purpose is and we understand that infinite intelligence is at our beck and call to realize our goals. Spirit informs us of what action to take. By keeping a healthy body, we can take meaningful and powerful action to pursue mental and spiritual goals. By understanding our mind – emotions and mental faculty – we keep our body healthy enough and we take the proper action to achieve results. Our results in turn allow us to engage with spirit, get feedback and determine the next best action to take. This is true with individuals, families, communities, businesses and large organizations.

Seventh Lotus Transformational Healing Center can help you understand this better and guide you and your organization to your goals through achieving health of the body, mind and spirit through workshops, seminars, retreats, and coaching. We look forward to being of service to you.

About Sraddha

Dr. Prativadi is the founder of Seventh Lotus Transformational Healing Center, a center dedicated to igniting human potential and catalyzing healing and wholeness to unlock higher performance and achievement in personal, professional and business settings.

Sraddha Prativadi, MD is a board-certified physician and surgeon specializing in Integrative Holistic Medicine and Women's Health. She currently practices in Rochester, New York. She is an assistant professor at a leading American medical school. She is an author, dancer and speaker who is sought after for her dynamic, engaging and inspiring presence. Her passion is helping individuals, groups and businesses achieve their potential by teaching skills and knowledge that allow maximization of the body, mind and connection to spirit, while being grounded in daily activities and measurable results.

She is a transformational consultant, using her expertise in human potential to help others unlock the power of their positive potential. With an extensive personal and cultural history in Eastern thought and holistic healing modalities, she employs an Integrative and holistic approach to her work in human potential.

She looks forward to connecting with you at:
DoctorP3.com and www.SeventhLotusTransformation.com.

CHAPTER 16

STOP SETTLING AND START THRIVING
A FIVE-STEP BLUEPRINT ON HOW TO ACHIEVE CAREER BLISS

BY LEEZA BYERS

If you don't know where you're going, any road will take you there.
~ Lewis Carroll, Alice in Wonderland

ARE YOU EAGER TO LIVE THE LIFE YOU DESERVE, YET JUST DON'T KNOW WHERE TO START?

Thousands of books have been written on the subject of finding one's purpose in life. Yet, a recent Mercer survey of 30,000 workers in 17 worldwide locations showed that 28% to 56% of employees wanted to leave their jobs. In the U.S. alone, 32% said they wanted to find new work. (Forbes, New Survey: Majority of Employees Dissatisfied.)

Why are so many people unhappy with their present careers? And, if they're so unhappy, why don't they do something about it? How many people do you know who are truly miserable in their jobs—and their jobs have just become a paycheck, and for some, not a great paycheck at that? They're not happy, they don't make enough money, they're not using their talents, and they've long since given up on finding their purpose or calling in life. Maybe I'm describing you!

You've probably felt a calling, but just haven't known what you can do from where you are. I've felt the same way and stood in your shoes—that moment was on March 20, 2008. I remember it vividly, because my husband and I were visiting with his grandmother in New York celebrating her 100th birthday. I happened to be on a train and saw this startling statistic – Only 3% of people ever find their true life's purpose!

This resonated with my spirit, as it immediately prompted me to ask myself if I was part of this small statistic. The answer, of course, was a resounding "no". Needless to say, this fact had me all wired up until we returned to our home in Georgia. I decided to embark on a personal quest to figure out what it is I needed to do, to become part of that 3% pack. I didn't want to be one of those people who never took the time or even made the effort to find out what my life's purpose is. I can tell you this much though, it wasn't an easy task. Most people who embark on this journey often become frustrated, as they struggle to figure out how to actually find their life's purpose.

However, five years later after having coached more than 1,000 professional women (and a few men in-between) and accumulating more than 7,000 hours of virtual and in-person coaching across the globe (including the UK, Trinidad, Thailand, Columbia, and of course, right here in the U.S.), combined with studying copious research that exists on the pursuit of happiness and success, I have seen firsthand that women who succeed at manifesting the desires of their heart have a few things in common. Likewise, I have had the privilege of observing some commonalities among women who struggle to achieve and sustain authentic success and happiness. Can you relate to any of these below?

Successful Women	Unsuccessful Women
A strong belief in their ability to handle obstacles when they come because the source of their strength comes from Christ	Give up at the onset of failure due to lack of a belief system.
A high propensity to take action and calculated risks	Are eternal procrastinators who won't get started because they fear failure and imperfection

Authenticity in setting their goals based on their deepest needs and desires	Allow society's standards to define their success rather than their own standards
A perspective on life that accepts failure and mistakes as a normal part of their journey in life	Work towards success as if it's a destination, a place where she will eventually "arrive"
A habit of saying "no" to what appears as "good" opportunities in favor of purposeful ones	Focus on what they don't have rather than what they do have

Whichever side of the table above that you ended up identifying yourself with, everyone at one point or another, stops what they're doing and wonders: "What on earth am I doing here?" Well, through the pages of this chapter, I will share as much as I can to help get you started on your own journey of answering this question. If you'd like to dive deeper than this chapter would allow, you can check for more of this good stuff on my website: www.leezabyers.com.

DEFINING SUCCESS

Let's first get a few definitions out of the way before moving forward. According to Webster's Dictionary, Success is defined as: "the accomplishment of an aim or purpose." If you analyze this definition with me, you may come to the realization that there may be more elements that make up the very essence of success itself. For me, I see success as a harmony of purpose, resilience, and, joy. Why? Simply put, success is living your life's purpose and embracing resilience and joy as you do. Now, let's break my definition down further.

YOUR PURPOSE OR YOUR CALLING – SHARING YOUR BLESSING

Wasn't there a high school or college counselor who said something to you about your calling once? Was it really that long ago that you last gave any thought to your purpose or calling in life? What do I even mean by that? Maybe you've heard of people having a "calling," a strong conviction toward a vocation, profession or vision, to do something in life that is meaningful to them. Everyone on this earth has an assignment or calling. You're not here just as a consumer (of air, water, food, etc.)

going through the motions, crossing off the days on a calendar. Yes, you have something unique that makes you special so you can share or bless others with. Whenever you give to others as an individual or a business, you are blessing them with something they need, desire or want. Your purpose in life answers a simple question: "How is someone's life better because she/he has crossed your path?" Better yet, ask yourself right now: "Who do I impact?"

Your Maker endowed you with gifts, talents, passions, and experiences that are unique to you. If I could travel back in time and observe you at 5 or 15 years old, I would see traces of your uniqueness. Your strengths have been with you all along, and now it's time for you to unleash them. There is a greater impact for you to make and now is the time to make it!

Purpose Exercise 1:

Take a few moments and give a concise, one-sentence answer to each of the following questions:

a)Who are you?

_____

b)What is your purpose in life?

_____

If you're like most of my clients, your answers describe what you do: *I'm an entrepreneur, I work in sales, I'm a teacher, I'm a doctor, a lawyer, a volunteer, a spouse, a parent,* etc. Of course, this list could go on and on, depending upon your job, hobbies, interests, or current role in life. All those answers may be perfectly valid, but remember, I asked, "Who are you?" **not** "What do you do?"

In today's culture, personal identity is most often defined by what we do. Beyond our jobs or roles in life, the majority of us don't have any idea who we are. This is especially true in the case of career professionals. They identify themselves solely as CEO, Top Sales Rep, District Manager, or some other title gained along the way. However, that's not the only place you see this happen. Look at the "empty nester syndrome" when children leave home. Some parents—particularly mothers—experience a lack of identity beyond this role that leaves them lost and occasionally even clinically depressed. I'll share a few other startling statistics that I came across. Did you know that: *1 in every 5 women is on anti-depressants* (not counting those who feel unhappy and unfulfilled); *6 out of 10 women can't sleep at night and experience overwhelming financial stress* (which is the #1 cause of chronic disease)?

This cultural norm of your job being your only identity can be a dangerous proposition. When it ends—and it will—you have no identity. That is why many of us have such a deep longing for purpose. Ask yourself these questions:

- *Do you believe somewhere in your soul that you know there's more to life than your job, role, or career?*

- *Wouldn't you agree that your life is about living a life of joy while we're here on this earth, and leaving a meaningful legacy when we're gone?*

The challenge is discovering that kind of purpose. So, finding a job or deciding to become a solo-preneur like myself, in a company culture that matches your style, is absolutely essential to getting the most fulfillment out of your life.

I've spent most of my adult life helping people in organizations reach their full potential and achieve higher levels of performance. For all of us, unleashing that potential depends, to a large extent, on how well we know ourselves—our goals, our talents, our values, and our personalities—and can apply that knowledge to *maximize our strengths* and *minimize our limitations*. If I've learned anything along the way, one thing is clear: Most of us want to be in a career where we experience **joy and feel satisfied that we contribute value to something bigger than ourselves.**

When you identify your purpose, you can leave fear, frustration, and fatigue behind. The first step in defining your purpose is to dig deep to unearth who you are, what you stand for and what you believe in. I'm going to share an excerpt from my Courageous Job Seekers & Entrepreneur Success System™ that I usually walk my clients through. Take a few moments and take as many lines you need to answer each of the following questions:

Step 1: CREATE YOUR VISION

Regardless of your current situation, write out your goals and your vision for your future. Better yet, you can even create a "Vision Board" which details your "image" for your new career your future life What you're doing, where it may take you, and what it means for you and your family can all be included.

My vision board is hanging in my office right where I can see it. It includes photos, testimonials and handwritten key phrases and goals! It keeps me on track and motivated!

The Vision for my Future is

_____

_____

Step 2: YOUR CAREER GOALS

My Career Goal Is

*Tip: You do not need to know HOW you are going to accomplish your goal! If you focus on the HOW you may get stuck. Just focus on what you want to accomplish—the HOW will work itself out.

_____

_____

My Driving Motivators Are:

*Tip: A driving motivator is a fixed, "I have to have this, no matter what" type need. *Examples include: relocating to another city, making a certain amount of money, or exiting a particular industry.* Most people generally have two to three driving motivators.

1) _____

2) _____

3) _____

Step 3: YOUR BRAND

What kind of work are you doing when you are loving the kind of work you do and at your very best? Once you have identified your "brand" you can "market" yourself authentically!

*Tip: Only concentrate on those skills and strengths you want to use in your next role/business.

I am loving my work when I:

_____

_____

My Brand Identity Is:

*Tip: What do others know and admire me for? What am I doing when I am "loving" my work?

_____

_____

My Choice Company & Title:

Describe the kind of company or business you envision yourself in (or who you're doing business with, if you decide to go into business for yourself), list all the components that are important to you! Is the environment traditional or casual? Academic? Cutting edge? Are you working in a high-rise downtown, working outside of town or telecommuting from your home? Writing these things down is going to help you in a number of ways.

My Choice Company Looks Like:

_____

_____

Step 4: VALUE PROPOSITION

What are the positive results you can promise your next employer or your clients (*if you decide to be an Entrepreneur*), and what problems do you solve? List ten so you can get really clear on your value and make sure you communicate these in your resume or on your website!

Tip: Your value proposition also includes your career achievements. Your career achievements explain what happens when you do what you do – so make sure you quantify wherever you can!

The secret to creating incredible career achievements is: to make sure your stories reflect those things you truly love to do the most, and to make sure your stories are quantified.

1._____   6._____

2._____   7._____

3._____   8._____

4._____   9._____

5._____   10._____

Step 5: YOUR MARKETING MATERIAL

Of course you are going to need a really well done resume and a value proposition letter ready to go (and a website if you're going to go into business for yourself)!

*Tip: Determine if you will design your resume/website yourself or if you should have your documents/website professionally designed.

RESILIENCE – WHERE IS YOUR FAITH?

As you set out in pursuit of your dreams, you will inevitably face challenges, trials, and tribulations along the way. However, it's how you handle these obstacles that will determine the outcome of your journey. What every successful woman already has in abundance is something called resilience. As Hebrews 11:1 reminds us, *"Faith is the confidence that what we hope for will actually happen; it gives us assurance about things we cannot see."* Do you have to be born with this trait? Absolutely not. Resilience is something anyone can develop through having faith, even if it is as little as a mustard seed (Luke 17:6).

Resilience Exercise #1:

Your assignment for the next 24 hours is to maintain a positive attitude. First, no matter how crazy it sounds, go to a mirror and yell out loud, **"I am great and I can do all things through Christ who strengthens me!"** Then, yell out the following phrases, **"I can do it!"** and **"I will get the job of my dreams!"** or if you're considering becoming a *'solopreneur'* or a *'mompreneur'* like me, then yell out: **"I will start the business of my dreams!"** Smile at yourself in the mirror while you are shouting out these affirmations. Second, for the next 24 hours, only try to be around positive people. If someone is negative around you, kindly remove yourself from the room or gently try to change the tone of the conversation to a positive tone. Finally, over the next 24 hours if anyone asks you how you are doing, just tell them "GREAT!" regardless of what's going on in your life at that time.

If you try this assignment over the next 24 hours, you will feel GREAT and you'll be ready to proceed with the next steps in finding your purpose-driven journey! I would be excited to know how this exercise turned out for you. So, feel free to connect with me on LinkedIn (just Google my name – Leeza Byers – and it's the first link that will pop up), so that you can share what you experienced with me personally.

SEIZE TODAY: TOMORROW MAY SUCK!

Based on knowledge and experience, you know you can change things by taking responsibility *(Be Proactive)*, knowing where you are going and why *(Begin with the End in Mind)* and prioritizing *(Put First Things First)*. Your next step is to let your *drive, passion* and *enthusiasm* propel you forward toward action. Develop a plan based on the previous steps shared in this chapter and then implement it. Plans mean nothing without implementation. Remember, champions become champions by doing. They maintain a discipline until it becomes a habit. Your daily actions will determine what is next for YOU. I'll see you at the top in that 3% club!

Favorite Quote that I share with My Courageous Job Seekers™ & Entrepreneurs™:

Be yourself. Everyone else is already taken.
~ Oscar Wilde

About Leeza

Leeza Byers is also known as **The Career Happy Expert**. Her lifelong passion is to help women achieve their maximum potential in life. She enjoys helping ambitious, career-minded women who sense that they were meant for a greater purpose, but are not quite sure on how to uncover and step into their true purpose. They are serious about having a career they love, that best matches their strengths and interests, and are ready to find their IDEAL career path ... their PURPOSE.

She is also a highly-sought-after speaker for top Economic Empowering events, to share her wealth of knowledge on marketing strategies for Executives and Mid-Career professionals in today's challenging economy. She has shared the stage with notable personalities such as: Michelle Singletary, Paula White, and Bishop TD Jakes. She has also been featured at "Female Success Factor" events in Atlanta, GA and is the Resident Career Expert for: *Women for Hire, Forbes Woman on LinkedIn,* and an *Atlanta Career Examiner.*

Leeza created the **Courageous Job Seeker Success System**™ and the **Courageous Entrepreneur Success System**™ out of a passion to assist ambitious, forward-thinking professionals – Executives and Mid-Career professionals. Her system also has a Christian component and is often the missing piece of a PURPOSE SEEKER'S puzzle. As Guisela I. mentioned: "Her easy coaching style and passion for helping others was evident from the start of working together."

Besides exploring their purpose, the women Leeza works with also want to regain that precious balance between work and their personal lives, so that they have a career they love at an income they deserve—and never have to suffer through another 'Life-Sucking' day at a job they hate.

- Books: *The Confident Woman: Tapping Into Your Inner Power* (2013)
- Publications: *Gallery of Best Resumes and Cover Letters* (2012)
- Nominations: *Unstoppable Woman* (2015)
- Awards: 3-time recipient of one of the most prestigious Awards in the Career Industry – the TORI (Toast of the Resume Writing Industry) for "Best Technical/ IT Resumes," "Best Sales & Marketing Executive Resumes," and "Best Cover Letters". (2011 and 2014)

CHAPTER 17

THE TORTOISE METHOD
—HOW TO RESET YOUR LIFE FOR GREATNESS

BY DESIREE ARAGON NIELSON

INTRODUCTION

Perhaps you've heard the fable of the tortoise and the hare. It is the tale of a hare who was so certain of his speed that he takes a nap mid-race. Meanwhile his challenger, the tortoise, diligently plods along at a much slower pace. Ultimately, the tortoise wins the race simply because the hare didn't wake up in enough time to cross the finish the line. Over the years, we've been told that it is noble and right to be the tortoise, to move steadily forward rather than be fast and careless. Yet, with advancements in technology and increased access to information, it feels like we're moving faster than ever. What lessons does this familiar fable have for us in this day and age?

It certainly seems like we are all running as fast as the hare. One client, an inspirational entrepreneur, expressed his frustration at having to travel for work and then come home and travel for his children's competitive sports teams. Weekends are filled with soccer and swim tournaments, wins and losses. Week days are filled with business decisions, sports practices and homework. Customers tell him what services to deliver, sports coaches tell him he has to meet volunteer requirements, and the school teachers want him to lead the children through the Math worksheets and English projects. He is running at full speed, yet there is still not enough of him to go around.

Then we have the personal fulfillment dilemma. We are faced with more research than ever before, telling us on how to live our best lives. We can read this book, learn about the value of body movement, healthy food intake, and emotional well-being. Yet, instead of feeling better, these easily accessible data points can actually make us feel worse. Another client, an energy artist, shared that she knows that she should be doing more for self-care, but feels as though there simply "isn't time" to work on her basic physical and emotional needs. She feels like if she stops long enough to take care of her basic needs then she will be letting somebody down. She is so busy tending to everyone else she is unable to actually do what's best for her overall well-being.

In Western culture, we seem to have become addicted to doing more and doing it faster and better than the rest. Addicted to being like the overly confident hare, our desire to get more done has caused many of us to lose sight of the deeper meaning in our actions and ultimately in our lives. Too many of us are habitually behaving as if there is a finish line, a destination to arrive at where we can be complete, done, finished. We're so attached to getting over the finish line that we forget that there really is no beginning or end. In our fable, the hare doesn't make it to the finish line and becomes the loser. But is it possible that maybe he really won something incredible? A fresh perspective? A humbling start of something new?

Maybe you are feeling a bit underwhelmed with your life? Or maybe you've achieved all of your set goals up to this point, but you're wondering if there is something more? This is where the tortoise can be our guide. In the fable, we celebrate the tortoise for winning the race through her diligence. Maybe, we've missed the vital factors that actually contributed to the success. What if the tortoise actually won long before she got to the finish line? What if the tortoise's real success came from just accepting the challenge set forth by the hare? We all know that traditionally, a hare is faster than a tortoise. It would have been so easy for the tortoise to simply walk away from the race altogether. But, the tortoise actually looked at the hare's challenge and saw an opportunity. Something new to try.

When it comes to personal growth, we're never really done. There is no final destination. Instead, we experience times of resetting. When the tortoise accepted the challenge, she reset herself from a common tortoise to a racing tortoise. . . . same inner self, new outward expression. And amazingly, in becoming a racer, our tortoise did not try to race like a hare. Instead, the tortoise brought all of her own unique skills and abilities to the race. She was diligent, thoughtful, and persistent in getting to the finish line, already knowing that this was just the start of her journey, not the end.

When we hold the belief that there is only one answer, one way to be, or one destination – we miss out. Thinking we need a quick fix (like traveling less, or magically getting more time) is just a way of avoiding our intrinsic truth. In reality, no matter how much success we achieve we may never feel fully satisfied. Like the tortoise and the hare, humans are meant to grow. We are designed to stretch beyond our comfort zones and introduce ourselves to new challenges. Despite the outward appearance, the clients introduced earlier were not frustrated by their circumstances, they were frustrated with their lack of growth. They were stuck in the status quo. The discomfort had become enough for them to seek out support and encouragement, but not so uncomfortable that they could immediately see where an outdated pattern was holding them back. Isn't this also what happened to the hare? He became so used to his capabilities, he just kept racing the same race and forgot the feeling of truly being challenged. In the absence of a real challenge, he began to look at his situation with frustration and contempt. H-m-m-m.

The hare, like so many of us, looked externally for a challenger. We want others to show us what's next. We buy into cultural norms, bigger houses, fancier cars, more possessions and lose sight of ourselves. Small moments of happiness begin to get replaced with obligations and responsibilities – mortgages, car payments, childcare, and clutter. They all require more and more time, attention and money. While these things may appease us momentarily, the feeling is fleeting.

Whatever success you have achieved up to this point, there is always room for growth. The opportunity for the most driven of us is to heed the call and step into the possibilities of greatness. It can be a little confusing to work so hard, to become competent and prove ourselves in one segment of our lives only to turn that upside down and start again. Imagine our tortoise telling her family of her plans to race the hare, "You're out of your mind!" they might say. Or, "Why would a tortoise want to race a hare?" The tortoise knew why. Having looked inside herself, the tortoise felt compelled to go beyond what had always been the norm – to go for something new.

Having earned a Master's Degree in Human Resources and Organizational Development, I spent over a decade coaching and consulting leaders to achieve peak performance. I held a Director-level position within a healthcare system and worked with the organization's Executives to grow and prepare the next generation of senior leadership. It was great, I was applying everything I'd learned up to that point, engaging in thoughtful dialogue, facilitating some of the best training content available, and watching leaders grow. One day, I began to notice that the work which I had previously loved, began to feel routine and unfulfilling. I had become the hare. My leaders were making great strides, but my sense of connection to the corporate process was fading.

After some period of self-reflection, I realized the challenge in front of me was one of acceptance for my love of intuition and spirituality. Up to that point, words like intuition and spirituality were undiscussables in the workplace, so I was holding back – refraining from giving all of myself to the work. A short time after this realization, I became aware of a Spiritual Life Certification program sponsored by the Emerson Institute. This year-long program taught practices for meditation, guided imagery, quantum inquiry, and mindfulness. Like the tortoise, I had to make a decision. Stay comfortable or accept the challenge of something new.

I went for the specialized certification and, while in pursuit, I was introduced to a visionary CEO who offered me an Executive position within her mission-driven bioscience company. The transition into the Executive position was a natural next step in my career. The work was intense and fast paced. By comparison, the coaching certification program had me doing work that was mindful and paced to match my client's natural rhythms.

The corporate work required action, action, action. The coaching work supported a variety of activities: self-reflection, mindfulness, and some big life-altering decisions. The corporate work required attention to staff at all levels of the organization, the coaching work allowed me to focus on one inspirational person at a time. It did not take long for me to reach yet another decision point. This time I more fully accepted the challenge. I reset and chose to make coaching inspirational people my full-time work. I still get to work with visionary Executives and now have the good fortune of also working with artists, authors and other creatives as well. Today, I am the happiest I've ever been.

My story, and those of my clients naturally align into three easy steps, referred to here as the Tortoise Method. When you feel this push to go beyond your existing circumstances, use the tortoise method to increase your sense of personal satisfaction and grow into an extraordinary life.

THE TORTOISE METHOD

1.   Reflect

Whatever your life circumstance up until now, it may have seemed easiest to just to keep on doing what you've always done. But there is a cost to this decision.You're missing out on aspects of your identity and actually increasing the likeliness of frustration or dissatisfaction setting in. When parts of yourself are left undiscovered or, worse yet abandoned, this is a guaranteed loss. We are meant to do so much more than live an ordinary life.

Our most effective lives come from the steady work of internal reflection. Our tortoise knew that that there was something more inside. Take time to consider how you got to your current life. Is every part of you being fully maximized? Constantly consider new possibilities.

2.   Accept

Once the pathways of self-awareness are open, we must then begin to take action. When the hare asked if anyone wanted to race, the tortoise was ready. Too often, we think that in order to live our best life we must make big, bold moves. What if in our organizations and our homes, we started with smaller more deliberate steps? Our tortoise did not quit everything she'd ever known, sell her shell and move to the Bahamas. Instead, our hero took one small step, she accepted the challenge of something new. We may never know whether the tortoise expected to win, but we do know that the win only became possible because of the single decision to step forward into the race.

When we accept the challenge and begin taking one small step at a time, new doors are sure to open. However, let's be real, if you have earned a partnership as a well-respected lawyer and have a dream to be an artist – not everyone in your life is going to jump for joy at the life changes that may come with following your heart's desire. Your loved ones will have questions. Heck, you'll have questions. Following our natural inclination for personal growth will definitely come with a bit of uncertainty.

Still, we have a responsibility to expect more from each other, but not in the "get-more- done" way to which we've become accustomed. Instead, we must dig deeper to continually uncover activities, career and love choices that give us a sense of meaning. The opportunity in our modern, technology-driven world is to be more of who we're meant to be, . . . to continue to grow beyond what has been tried before, . . . to excel beyond what our predecessors and ancestors set in motion long ago. We can only do this successfully if we accept the challenge, whenever it arises.

3. Reset

To the best of our knowledge, our tortoise had never raced before but she carried a desire in her heart to be in the race. The road ahead was fraught with uncertainty. Would the tortoise be accepted by loved ones? Were there resources to support the racers? What would happen if an injury occurred? These are all reasonable questions but none that stopped our hero. She took her expertise as a tortoise and followed her heart, resetting herself into a racing tortoise.

Remember our traveling Dad mentioned earlier in the chapter. Sure, he felt busy, but at his core, the real issue was that he had a deep unmet desire to write. His work and sense of responsibility had become his reason for not acting on something he'd always wanted to do. In his case, he also worried about the quality of his writing. Between work, family and fears, he'd subconsciously made the decision not to write anything at all. When he rediscovered this long-forgotten desire, he was able to tap into his love of the written word. Rather than setting a goal to have a best seller, which kept him stalled and frustrated, this dad simply began to schedule small chunks of time to work on his writing. This single decision to reset himself into a writer only took a few hours a week, could be done while traveling, and re-ignited passion into every aspect of his life.

CONCLUSION

The tortoise did not win by being more efficient, more driven or even more confident than the hare. She did not have a better life coach, a better fitness trainer, more time or more money than the hare. She just had a strong desire for something new. She reflected on the intrinsic truth of her identity, accepted the challenge presented by the hare and reset her life one deliberate step at a time. Ultimately, she won. In today's world, we have access to more technology and more information than ever before. For the well-being of humanity, it is vital that we slow down just long enough to tap into what we need and want for a meaningful life, continuously seek out opportunities for personal growth and joyfully accept new challenges.

Ready. Set. Go!

About Desiree

Desiree Aragon Nielson serves as an inspirational coach, card reader and speaker based out of beautiful Northern California. As a mother, wife, daughter, friend and former Executive, she helps inspirational people tap into their greatness and see things in a remarkably positive light.

In healthcare, Desiree was instrumental in the implementation of an executive-level succession planning process. She designed an award-winning healthcare Leadership program for emerging executives. Desiree uses this experience developing people in combination with her abilities to intuitively communicate. Desiree recognizes that given the public nature of their work, inspirational people are expected to be "on" all the time. Artists, authors, and visionary business executives are always being watched. And, they are frequently faced with the challenge of living authentically while sustaining their powerful influence. Desiree partners with inspired people to process difficult situations and grow themselves into greatness.

Desiree is passionate about making our lives more joyful. She has an uncanny ability to pick up on subtle nuances which allow her to quickly show inspirational people fast changes they can make to manifest bliss back in their lives. It has always been easy for Desiree to lift up others so they can fully see and maximize their potential. Desiree has designed and delivered retreats and workshops for audiences in Asia, Canada, Costa Rica, and throughout the United States. In individual, group and large event settings.

Desiree has developed hundreds of inspirational people across a wide variety of industries, including artists, authors and CEO's of fast-growing companies. Desiree has been certified to train and facilitate premier leadership programs, deliver difficult messages, and influence with persuasion. She is also a Certified Spiritual Life Coach. Desiree is a member of the Women's Speakers Association (WSA) and an active member of the National Association of Women Business Owners (NAWBO).

People are attracted to Desiree's strong ability to synthesize complex qualitative ideas while easily connecting with their ultimate intention. And, Desiree is attracted to inspirational people who desire to use their innate gifts to have a positive impact on our world. These factors make it Desiree's personal mission to provide inspirational people with uplifting dialogue so they can think and grow out of the ordinary and into the extraordinary.

You can connect with Desiree at:
- https://www.instagram.com/desiree_aragon_nielson
- https://www.linkedin.com/in/desireenielson
- https://www.facebook.com/desireearagonnielson

CHAPTER 18

SLAVE TO LOVE

BY GLEN JAKOB MANDALINIC

We must let go of the life we have planned,
so as to accept the one that is waiting for us.
~ Joseph Campbell

THE BEGINNING – BABY STEPS

We find it very difficult to start to write at all without being grateful to Nick Nanton, Brian Tracy and all the people behind the scenes that we take for granted for the process of metamorphosis. This is what dreams are made of – this time it's not Iowa. All those voices in your head. It's a fine, tethered line between success and insanity. We don't have to tell you. When I begin to go insane, I take baby steps. I acknowledge my breath – the giver and taker of life. In those moments, I realize I am nothing, yet everything. One of those voices led me here.

PART 1 – THE END OF INNOCENCE

When I was 7, my father took me to see my best friend one night at some place I had never seen before. She was 6. I was happy for some reason as I hadn't seen her for a while – she was our next-door neighbour – and she was in hospital for a while. We weren't playing in the backyard these days. Things weren't the same anymore. So, we get to this place, I ran inside and ran straight to the casket – passing these people crying and wearing black. It hadn't dawned on me. . .
Anxiously, and in anticipation of catching up with Suzy, I grabbed

the box she was in and leaned over into it. Bang! My brain exploded. This was not Suzy, she never wore heavy duty make up. I stayed awake that night until I couldn't stay awake anymore, under the shelter of the blankets. I don't remember the next day. Everything was a blur after that. All the decades that followed blended into one moment in time. From the confusion was born a fusion.

PART 2 – THE JOURNEY BEGINS – THE WIZARD OF OZ

Suzy woke me up.

We (me and my voices) commenced a journey, consummating periods of numbness and enlightenment, suffering and joy to succumb to the beginning once again. We were going around in circles. We have feelings that we don't like, and are puzzled in a juxtaposition of ambiguity and helplessness as to why we have them. We don't want them. Yet we have them. Are we putting too much emphasis on the wrong knob? The voices in my mind hijacked me. I lost the plot. I crumbled to the cold tile floor. I had no one, but at the same time, it felt as though I had everyone and everything – every tree, every branch, every ocean, every wave, every star, every blade of grass. Some force picked me and my voices back up again. This went on for many years. We had to unlearn to learn … and I was a very slow learner.

PART 3 – ADAM AND EVE

One day, the Lord came to Adam and said … "I've got some good news & some bad news." Adam looked at the Lord and said, "Well give me the good news first." Smiling, the Lord explained, "I've got two new organs for you, one is called a brain, the other a penis. The brain will allow you to be very intelligent and have intelligent conversations with Eve. The penis will allow you to reproduce intelligent life form on this planet. Eve will be very happy that you now have this organ to give her children." Adam, very excited, exclaims! "These are great gifts you have given me. What could possibly be bad news after such bad tidings?" The good Lord looked upon Adam and said, "When I created you, I only gave you enough blood to operate one of those organs at a time." ~ Anonymous.

PART 4 – MOTHER NATURE HAS THE LAST WORD

Life asked Death: "Why do people love me but hate you?" Death responded: "Because you are a beautiful lie and I am a painful truth." ~ Author Unknown.

No one wants to die. Even people who want to go to heaven don't want to die to get there. And yet death is the destination we all share. No one has ever escaped it. And that is as it should be, because Death is very likely the single best invention of Life. It is Life's change agent. It clears out the old to make way for the new.
~ Steve Jobs

PART 5 – ROUND UP THE USUAL SUSPECTS

At the beginning of your film there are many voices, by the end of your film there are only two – they eventually became one, and finally, one with nature. Just like in the movies.

PART 6 – WISHBONE OR BACKBONE

New York City can be the loneliest place on the planet and at times things can spiral downwards very quickly. And when the beer runs out, the piano man stops singing and the bar closes, you only have yourself and your voices with the cold wind biting on your face. But one voice stood out this night – Franky's voice, sharing his grandfather's wisdom that was passed onto him. He said, "Glen, I found in life, that to get through it more comfortably – it is better to have a backbone than a wishbone." Thank you, Franky, for being a light in those dark times. I never forgot. That changed the course of my life once again.

PART 7 – LEARNING TO WALK AGAIN

It is not enough to be busy. So are the ants.
The question is, what are we busy about?
~ Henry David Thoreau

1. If you can 'kill a thought dead', for that fleeting moment you can do anything. And therefore, this power is valuable if not epic. Not only will it free you from mental torment, but it gives you a concentrated

power absolutely unknown to you before. How do you do this? Practice breathing with total awareness. Otherwise, it's just a dream.

2. Acknowledge yourself from time to time. Listen to yourself breath. Give him/her a name. They are part of your make up. Acknowledge your other self. The other you. Introduce yourself to one another. It will be the beginning of a wonderful relationship. Talk to them in the mirror. Look him/her in the eye whenever you remember. Get along with them.

3. Your heart beats if you listen. *The heart has a brain.* ~ Gregg Braden

4. I get lazy with my mouth – so breathe through the nostrils only, it's all good. In fact – I found out the hard way – the more one keeps their mouth shut, the sooner the results surface. *Once a wise man said nothing.* ~ Buddha.

5. *Nostrils. Breathe Maverick. You can do this. Don't be a Goose.* ~ Tony Scott – Top Gun.

6. "They only see the glory – they never see the story."

7. To breathe consciously is to look at yourself in the mirror of your soul. It's in this position, with practice, that the answers start to appear to all those questions that you have asked.

8. Before you can really ever love anyone – it helps so much to love yourself first. That one had me stumped for a decade . . . two or three. *I beat it.* – Laline – Carlito's Way.

9. Be patient, for some it will take days, for others months, and yet others – years. I fall into the 'years' category.

10. If you can't do the above – then do it in a way that works for you. And go easy on the people that walk over you. Sometimes they are the ones that need the most love. They probably just don't know how to put it into words.

11. "If you are not evolving you are just revolving." ~ GJM

12. Nostril Awareness/Nostril Art. "The art of breathing is the art of life." ~ GJM
    Unconscious breath = Unconscious life.

13. *In the end, people will judge you anyway, so don't live life impressing others, live your life impressing yourself.* E. Infante.

PART 8 – REBEL WITHOUT A CAUSE

Here's to the crazy ones, the misfits, the rebels, the troublemakers, the round pegs in the square holes... the ones who see things differently – they're not fond of rules. You can quote them, disagree with them,

glorify or vilify them, but the only thing you can't do is ignore them, because they change things. They push the human race forward, and while some may see them as the crazy ones, we see genius, because the ones who are crazy enough to think that they can change the world are the ones who do.
~ Steve Jobs.

PART 9 – CONCLUDING THE JOURNEY

This journey isn't easy. But the destination is in sight. Just look up at the night sky.

PART 10 – "A LOVE LETTER TO MY CHILDREN"

When I proposed the theory of relativity, very few understood me, and what I will reveal now to transmit to mankind will also collide with misunderstanding and prejudice in the world.

I ask you to guard the letters as long as necessary, years, decades, until society is advanced enough to accept what I will explain below.

There is an extremely powerful force that, so far, science has not found a formal explanation to. It is a force that includes and governs all others, and is even behind any phenomenon operating in the universe and has not yet been identified by us.

This universal force is LOVE. When scientists looked for a unified theory of the universe they forgot the most powerful unseen force.

- ❖ *Love is Light, that enlightens those who give and receive it.*
- ❖ *Love is gravity, because it makes some people feel attracted to others.*
- ❖ *Love is power, because it multiplies the best we have, and allows humanity not to be extinguished in their blind selfishness.*
- ❖ *Love unfolds and reveals.*
- ❖ *For love we live and die.*
- ❖ *Love is God and God is Love.*

This force explains everything and gives meaning to life. This is the variable that we have ignored for too long, maybe because we are afraid of love because it is the only energy in the universe that man has not learned to drive at will.

To give visibility to love, I made a simple substitution in my most famous equation.

If instead of E = mc2, we accept that the energy to heal the world can be obtained through love multiplied by the speed of light squared, we arrive at the conclusion that love is the most powerful force there is, because it has no limits.

After the failure of humanity in the use and control of the other forces of the universe that have turned against us, it is urgent that we nourish ourselves with another kind of energy...

If we want our species to survive ... if we are to find meaning in life ... if we want to save the world and every sentient being that inhabits it, love is the one and only answer.

Perhaps we are not yet ready to make a bomb of love, a device powerful enough to entirely destroy the hate, selfishness and greed that devastate the planet.

However, each individual carries within them a small but powerful generator of love whose energy is waiting to be released. When we learn to give and receive this universal energy, dear Lieserl, we will have affirmed that love conquers all and is able to transcend everything and anything, because love is the quintessence of life.

I deeply regret not having been able to express what is in my heart, which has quietly beaten for you all my life. Maybe it's too late to apologize, but as time is relative, I need to tell you that I love you and thanks to you, I have reached the ultimate answer!

Your father,
Albert Einstein

Thanks for sharing this path with us. You are a bright ray of sunshine. Please indulge me and let me return the sentiment with these words from Sigmund Freud that woke me up - "Before you diagnose yourself with depression or low self-esteem, first make sure you are not, in fact, surrounded by assholes."

Hope is a good thing.

If you are not evolving you are just revolving.
~ Glen J Mandalinic

About Glen

Things happen to us whether we are conscious or not, but when we are unconscious, life has no meaning, so many people come to me without any idea of what it all means. People need an understanding of things, of why they live... ~ CG Jung

These "things" mentioned above are ubiquitous. They form 'the norm'. When we consistently question life, sooner or later we arrive at the perimeter of the awakening process born from the repetition of these four words "Why am I here?" ~ GJM

Glen Jakob Mandalinic's formal education in the university environment triggered an avalanche for further inquiry into what *Star Trek* coined "the new frontier."

Glen sought out masters of their craft, both home and abroad, in the field of human potential, including Bob Proctor, Brian Tracy, Dr. John DeMartini, Gregg Braden, Dr. Bruce Lipton, Neil DeGrasse Tyson, Esther Hicks, Louise Hay, NASA Astronaut Chris Hadfield, NRL legend Tommy Raudonikis, Dennis Waitley and Francis Pilchesky, to grasp a deeper intimacy into the universe of the mind that rests between his ears.

Glen is no guru, healer, preacher or teacher, just an awakened breather. If just for once, you really - STOP - BREATHE - LISTEN – RINSE - REPEAT - you will come to the road less travelled. And you will know that you are on that road when you come to a sign that reads:

Things don't have to be this way.
The resolution lies in the illusion. ~ GJM

Website:
www.youknowmorethanyouthink.com

CHAPTER 19

PREPARE FOR DEPARTURE – THE ABCs OF WINNING

BY WYNETT ISLEY

"Flight attendants, prepare for departure." It was the 1980s, many years before the tragic events of 9/11. I was traveling the northeastern United States for the National Disaster Medical System, serving as a contingency planner. Flying out of Chicago O'Hare airport heading to New England, I settled into my seat in the rear of the packed plane. The soothing voice of the flight attendant began telling us the expected flight time and the weather at our destination before beginning the pre-departure safety briefing. Suddenly a passenger near the front of the plane jumped up from his seat and yelled. "Portland, Maine? I want to go to Portland, *Oregon*!"

What a kerfuffle! Of course, the flight attendants helped the passenger off the plane. Our east-bound flight was only slightly delayed while they removed his luggage from the belly of the aircraft, and re-directed them to the west coast. After the excitement settled down, I made it to my destination with no more surprises.

As a planner, I wondered how that guy's preparations went wrong. What were the decision points, the action steps, the choices made that nearly led to his traveling to exactly the wrong destination? Had he prepared well? He thought he was ready, all set, on his way. Then he heard a voice telling him in a single syllable (*Maine*) that he needed to take immediate action. And, what about you? Where are you headed? Are you sure? Are you going where you intend to go? Are you prepared? Do you need a gentle voice clearly revealing the end point of your current path? Are you prepared to change your plans and take action to get on the right track?

For many years as a coach/consultant, I have had the privilege of helping individuals and organizations decide with clarity where they want to go, and create action plans to achieve their clearly-stated goals. Sometimes the process seems complicated, complex and confusing. That's why individuals and organizations hire someone like me, to facilitate their journey through the improvement process. A good coach knows that success starts with a goal, a plan, and knowledge and skill in the fundamentals. There are many techniques and tactics in the coaching toolbox; we work to make the complex understandable and actionable. In my practice, I use a simple formula to explain and reinforce the fundamentals of success: A -> B -> C.

The "A" stands for Attitude, the mindset and invisible aspects we bring to each situation. The "B" stands for Behavior, the observable actions we take, the things we do. The "C" stands for Consequences, the results, whether by design or by default. It's an axiom that your current process is exquisitely designed to give you exactly the results you're currently getting. Thinking you can continue to do the same things and get a different result is the definition of insanity. If you're not getting the results you want, you need to apply the ABCs of Winning, the formula for success:

$$A \longrightarrow B \longrightarrow C$$

Let's work our way backwards from the "C" as we explore this success formula. What consequences do you desire? Where do you want to go? What do you want to achieve? Can you see it clearly enough to create a picture in someone else's mind? Do you have a vivid Vision? Sometimes the most difficult decision is to decide what you want, to determine your next goal as you discover your life's purpose, your calling, your passion, your Vision.

If you decline to choose the consequences you desire, you'll end up living by default instead of design. Make a deliberate decision. Choose a compelling future. In my practice, I teach my clients the tools, techniques and tactics for success. The success technology is like electricity. Electricity doesn't care what appliance is connected; when you flip the switch, the energy flows. Committing to a goal, any goal, provides the switch that activates the formula.

After you choose a desired consequence, shift left from the "C" to the "B" in the success formula. With your chosen goal in mind, review whether your current behaviors are effective to achieve that goal. Commit to becoming your best. The knowledge about "how" to move from the current state to the desired future state is available in the universe. A mentor, teacher or coach can help determine which strategies, tactics and techniques will get you to the goal. Gathering data helps avoid self-deception.

We need to be honest and clear about where we currently are, with facts and data as well as feelings and thoughts. Like the traveler on the plane, we know we got on a plane in the middle of the continent, and we might think we're headed in the right direction only to discover, when we gain objective clarity, just how far off target our current course of action will take us. Acknowledging the distance between where we are and where we want to be, we can design our path, and make adjustments when we discover we're off course. We can set milestones to measure our progress and we can prepare for contingencies.

The Consequences you are experiencing, the conditions, circumstances and situations in which you find yourself today are the result of processes, systems, behaviors and habits. The result you have is the result of what you've done, what you've allowed, where you've been. So where do you find yourself just now? Do you find yourself on a plane headed to the wrong coast, 3,000 miles in the opposite direction from what you desire? That's a long way off from the goal. Without a willingness to receive honest data, we continue to do what we're doing, to behave like we're used to behaving. Will your current habits and patterns of behavior result in your chosen goal? Are your actions by design or by default? Are you willing to change?

The idea that where you are today is the result of the things you've done yesterday and previously, that the consequences are the result of your behavior, might be a new concept. Where you are right now as you listen to this, as you read this, as you watch this, is the result of a set of behaviors, of habits. You clicked a link. You opened the book. You did something to get something. Believe in your ideal self. We achieve intentional success when we choose our consequences and change our behavior to take action that moves toward the chosen goal. Begin now.

As a life coach, a business performance improvement facilitator, a management consultant and as an organizational coach, I invite my clients to explore, to dream, to discover this simple formula: $A \rightarrow B \rightarrow C$. The results, the "what you have right now" consequences or the "C" in the formula is the result of habits, patterns and behaviors, the "B" factor; and behind the behavior action or inaction is the "A" factor, the Attitudes underlying our behavior. Why do we do what we do? Why do you do what you do? What are the underlying factors for the behavior that created the consequence? Using techniques like storytelling and values clarification, we can explore the question beyond "what are you doing?" to the deeper question "why do you that?"

Sometimes our behaviors and actions are effective and functional and clearly support progress toward the chosen goal. Sometimes our actions seem like self-sabotage. We know what would be effective, we know what we should do, but we don't do it. We don't behave in a manner that supports progress toward our goal. Instead our action or inaction blocks our progress. We don't make that call. We miss the deadline. We eat the junk food. We go on a spending spree. The formula for success invites us to explore three factors – Consequences, Behaviors, and Attitudes.

The formula invites us to explore the "A" factor through honest self-examination, into what is hidden, into the mindset behind the behaviors. Honestly acknowledge your attitudes, and accept yourself. Often hidden from ourselves are our attitudes, beliefs, paradigms, perspectives, and unconscious patterns of how we see the world, the mindset that creates the frame for what we expect. These attitudes are the "A" factor in our formula. All of us hold within ourselves thought patterns in which we believe we know how the world ought to be, what should be, how it works. It takes effort to reveal the attitudes, the beliefs, the emotions and feelings that shape your interaction with the external world.

Sometimes it is helpful when an objective person serves as a mirror to reveal what we can't see for ourselves. With the help of another, we can explore together and discover the "A" – attitudes – that create the "B" – behaviors – that create the "C" – consequences. When our attitudes are revealed, we can decide if we want to change them. We can challenge our beliefs. Some of the typical blocking beliefs are: "I'm too young." "I'm too old." "They won't let me." "It's too hard." "That's how they are." By exposing our beliefs, we can decide if they serve us well, or if they are erroneous and need to be changed. The American psychologist William James revealed, "The greatest discovery of my generation is that a human being can alter his life by altering his attitudes."

What do you believe? How do you behave? What is the life you would love living? What are the consequences you want? You want to win. You want to succeed. You want to be successful. Advocate for your growth and development. Start by stating explicitly the desired consequence. To minimize the chance that we'll get a rude awakening like our hapless traveler, we need to clearly state that we want Portland in Maine or we want Portland in Oregon, or maybe we want to visit both and we clarify the desired sequence and length of time in each wonderful location.

Saying we want to win or saying we want more is insufficient clarity. We must define what it means to "win" in objective terms, so there is no misunderstanding, no ambiguity, no buying a ticket to the wrong destination. Do you want to go east or west? North or south? Start simple. The four cardinal points on the compass are a good starting point. Maybe you don't want to go north, maybe you want to go South-by-Southwest. You can choose any direction, any destination. Begin with the end in mind, the "C" in the formula. Set a target, a desired destination, define your dream. Begin by defining the desired consequence, the "C" in the ABCs of Winning.

In business, the desired consequence is to increase revenue, to increase profits. The specific target might be to increase revenue by 10% or the target might be a specific revenue or profit number. The financial consequence goal is specific, measurable and objective. In business, there are accountants and financial officers and chief executives who know the numbers. By clearly defining the desired future state, we can objectively measure our current situation so we can plan the journey from where we are to where we want to be.

The ABCs of Winning formula applies in the business environment very well. Start with the end in mind, the "C" consequence, then investigate the "B" behaviors, the processes, the systems, the operations that create the product or service that the customer buys to generate revenue, then develop the company culture, the "A" attitudes that are revealed in the behaviors that create the desired consequence.

For an individual, the formula works the same. Begin by defining the "C" state. Perhaps you have a financial target, a desired future state, a money consequence. Be specific. If you say you want "more," I will hand you a penny, and you will immediately have more than you had a moment earlier. Congratulations, you're a winner! Was that what you meant? Was that what you had in mind? Be specific.

Many people begin their exploration of the success formula with a desire for financial freedom. Refine that into a specific, objective, clearly defined goal, in both external measures like dollars, and internal measures like the feeling that accompanies achieving that desired state. Would having a million dollars make you feel safe and secure? What do you believe about money? Attitude drives behavior which creates consequences. If you learn what to do, will you do it? The "C" consequence we want is the result of a pattern of "B" behaviors, a sequence of events, habits and patterns of performance based on what we are willing and capable of doing.

Knowledge and skill can be learned to bridge the capability gap from where we are to where we want to be. Before you leap into action, ponder the possible consequences. Imagine having achieved the goal, and consider whether it is what you truly desire. As human beings, we have the capacity for imagination. When you are a millionaire, what specifically happens during your ideal day? What time do you wake up? What does your bedroom look like? How does it feel? How does it smell? What do you eat for breakfast? How do you spend your day? What are the daily behaviors of you, the millionaire? Are you prepared to be a millionaire? What do you need to know? Where can you gain that knowledge? What might hold you back? What conditions require attention? Is your goal crystal clear and unambiguous?

When the goal was vague, such as "more money" and one penny was added, was that what you had in mind? What did you have "in mind" when you were forming the goal in your thoughts, in your beliefs, in your emotions? It's important to discover what you have in your mind because your attitudes, beliefs, emotions, paradigms and thoughts drive you to particular behaviors. Those behaviors become habits when they are repeated often enough with sufficient emotional intensity. Be intentional about your behavior and the consequence is assured.

So, I invite you to explore the ABCs of your current situation, the ABCs of Winning. If you're ready, let's go. If you need support, ask. Get ready. Discover your dream. Set your destination. Decide for the consequence you desire. Becoming self-aware of attitudes, beliefs and paradigms is a skill that requires practice. Being intentional about behavior and building good habits that create desired results is a skill that requires practice. Learning to navigate the **ABC**s of Winning is achievable.

A:

- Accept yourself.
- Acknowledge your attitudes.
- Advocate for your growth and development.

B:

- Believe in your ideal self.
- Book calendar time for improvement activities.
- Begin now.

C:

- Create a vivid Vision.
- Choose a compelling future.
- Commit to becoming your best.

The fundamental factors in the formula for success are Attitudes, Behaviors, Consequences. Now you know the ABCs of Winning. Now is your time.

Get ready. Prepare for departure. Let's go!

About Wynett

Wynett Isley is a professional facilitator, life mastery consultant, performance improvement coach, author and trainer. Wyn brings a wealth of experience serving a wide variety of industries to her elite clientele of senior executives, top performers, and dedicated self-development practitioners.

Wyn knows how it feels to face the decision to either quit or dig deep and begin again. Whether your current situation is through design or default, Wyn can masterfully guide you through the process of learning and practicing the necessary tools, techniques and tactics to hit the 'reset' button and get on the right path to discover and live into your greatness now.

Her areas of expertise include quality management, leadership development, team collaboration, performance excellence, strategic management, employee engagement, and individual personal and professional development. Wyn has two Master's degrees, a graduate certificate in National Strategic Studies, and numerous certificates in coaching, consulting and performance development. She has served as adjunct faculty for several graduate schools, and holds membership in numerous professional associations.

With discretion and rigorous compassion, Wyn has supported clients ranging from multi-billion dollar global enterprises, not-for-profit organizations, and veterans' groups, to sincere individuals who want to [re]discover their dream, and learn the technology that supports their designing and living a life they love, achieving greater success in their personal and professional lives.

CHAPTER 20

READY, SET, GO ENJOY YOUR LIFE!

BY VIOLET DETRE

INTRODUCTION

If you are reading this, I applaud you. That means you want some type of change in your life. Maybe you need motivation, encouragement, or would like to see progress. Or perhaps you feel like life is rushing by, and you don't have time to slow down. Maybe you're spending too much time 'in your head.' What is missing in your life? Is it joy, peace, or fulfillment? Sometimes these can seem elusive. Sometimes you think those precious things will have to wait until (*fill in the blank*). Truth be told, you'll feel better by not outsourcing your happiness, you can choose to enjoy your life now.

First, I will tell you an abridged part of my story. Then, I will share some practices I've used to feel more at peace and enjoy my life in the midst of life's challenges, those things that come up for which we need to make adjustments, the unwanted things that we wish wouldn't occur.

A LITTLE BACKGROUND TO MY STORY

About four years ago, I found myself in a fight for my life. I had been struggling with health issues since I was a teen. From the outside, I seemed alright. I was an honors student (part of the gifted and talented program) since the third grade and did well in school. Doctors didn't think anything was wrong. However, I knew my energy levels were not up to par. In fact, I could fall asleep at the drop of a hat. Although I wanted to exercise, I didn't have the energy to. People didn't think much of it, dismissing it as genetic. I had memory issues, pain walking or standing for any length of time, and what some thought were seasonal illnesses

"Maybe it was all in my head," I thought. My symptoms worsened as the years went by. But, since the "experts" dismissed my symptoms, other than asking for prayer from as many people as I could, I tried to ignore my ailments. That is until an eye-opening occurrence in 1998, while living overseas because my husband, a service member with the U.S. Army, was stationed there due to a deployment. My brother Juan (whom we call Wil) and my younger sister, Lily, came to visit and enjoy a European vacation with us. One day, my sister asked me about an activity we had done the day prior. But try as I could, I could not remember the event or those around it. My sister exclaimed, "Violeta!" my birth name, in a very concerned tone. Finally, someone had noticed that it was not normal! So, I started to be more concerned about my deteriorating health.

That realization led me on a quest to find solutions. The hospital ended up almost like my second home, yet the medical tests failed to pinpoint any specific diagnosis. Eventually, the frustration and disillusionment took over. I was fatigued, in pain, and sick repeatedly. It was difficult to function, much less hold a job. I was too tired to work, and domestic responsibilities have never been my strong suit nor something I found fulfilling. This was not how I had envisioned my life. Growing up I was told I would be a success. But instead, I felt utterly useless. "What good am I?" I thought. There were glimmers of hope in between. For example, some prescription medication helped at first. However, eventually, they worsened my condition.

THE PERFECTIONISM PLAGUE

Health issues were not my only limitation. Perfectionism also had its hand in my dissatisfaction with myself and with life. I've always had high expectations of myself, my surroundings, and of life in general. This is not to say that setting high expectations is wrong, but it is counterproductive when they are unrealistic. Needless to say, this desire to be perfect was a heavy burden for me. It added to my frustration and left me feeling hopeless.

STRUGGLES WITH SELF-PITY

Through it all, I tried to make God and church a priority. But, I became disappointed with God because it didn't seem like He was coming through for me. I sought help from professional counselors, which didn't help much. Looking back, it may have been because it made me feel as if there was something wrong with me, which compounded the negative feelings I was having about myself.

MY CHOICE TO LIVE WITH MORE POSITIVITY

Thank God for naturopathic doctors. Their tests finally revealed all sorts of issues including adrenal fatigue, brain fog, and immunity issues from heavy metal toxicity. Additionally, I had contracted mold toxicity somewhere along the line. By this time, I was also displaying signs of neuropathy and could barely stay awake during the day no matter how much caffeine I consumed. I felt God tell me that I would not die from my current condition. Also, I had heard that doctors encourage patients with terminal diseases to fight the disease using positivity. I knew then that I had a choice to follow that advice or be negative and feel painfully miserable, which would probably affect my healing process as well.

So, I made the decision to make a consistent effort to try to stay positive. Like Jesse Duplantis says, "I tried [it], and I didn't like it!" (Trinity Broadcasting Network, 2015, 0:57). I had lived in utter depression and my self-imposed prison of negativity long enough!

MY DESIRE FOR YOU

One of the biggest impacts of my recovery and helping me to transition to my betterment were some strategies I learned to implement over time, some of which I'm sharing below. You can implement these as well and know that no matter what you're going through today, you too can have victory in your life. Though I'm still under my naturopathic doctor's care, my health has drastically improved. I have completed grad school and am starting my thriving coaching business. Most of all, I am more at peace and trying to make the most of everyday. *I urge you, don't postpone enjoying your life.* Enjoying your life now will help you reach that pinnacle of success with more ease—that is my desire for you.

A FEW STRATEGIES FOR ENJOYING YOUR LIFE

1. _Breathe deeply_ – Not just a breath that fills your lungs, but one that takes a steady count to five or seven, that makes you stand or sit taller, and fills your abdomen as well. In the article, "Relaxation Techniques: Breath Control Helps Quell Errant Stress Response," the author states that deep breathing, or diaphragmatic breathing, has multiple benefits including reducing stress, lowering or stabilizing blood pressure, and improved immunity.

2. _Reduce tension_ – The author also says that most of us do not fill up all our lungs with the shallow breaths we normally take. I realized I was guilty of mostly taking shallow breaths. Throughout my life I was uptight and tense. But the simple technique of breathing deeply helped me to relax and feel so much better right away. Try it now, slowly inhale through your nose filling as much of your lungs and diaphragm/belly as you can, exhale slowly, relax as you let go of all tension. Try this a few times and during breaks throughout your day.

   Breathing deeply is a great start, but adding conscious muscle relaxation increases the impact. After you take a couple of deep breaths, start breathing normally. Be aware of how your body feels starting from the top of your head down. Are there any specific areas that you felt tension? Make a conscious effort to try to relax those areas throughout the day.

   I am usually most tense in my shoulders and jaw. For some people, it may be their stomach area where they hold most of their stress. Sometimes, if I'm having trouble sleeping, I go through the tension reduction exercise above, and find out I'm tense in all sorts of places. So, try it before sleeping, as well.

3. _Celebrate your successes!_ – Positive psychologists have ascertained that "savoring experiences . . . is one key to happiness." (Moore, 2010, para. 11). I have to admit, this is one that I'm still working on incorporating more of into my life. Relishing in the feeling of having accomplished, learned, done something well, or even for being you reminds you of the magnificent and capable human being you are! It creates milestones to remind yourself of how you exhibited greatness in the past.

It can also serve as a driving force when you look forward to feeling that way after a challenging goal or project. Remember to do it with enthusiasm. So, give yourself a high-five, jump, dance, whatever gets you pumped—celebrate you!

4. *Positivity* – Positivity makes you smarter. In fact, research shows that for people with a positive mind-set, performance on nearly every level—productivity, creativity, engagement—improves (Achor, 2012). Did you know that you can choose your thoughts? Yes, you have that power! The Bible says, "as a man [or woman] thinks in his [or her] heart so is he [or she]." (Prov. 23:7, New King James Version)

Essentially, your thoughts drive you, can potentially affect your emotions, and subsequently your actions. If you want a happy life, develop a positive mindset. A way to begin doing this is to repeat positive affirmations.

5. *Gratitude!* – For years, Jose (aka Joe) would urge me to be thankful. Although he tends to have copious amounts of nuggets of wisdom, for some reason I was resistant to making it a continual practice. It took me years to realize how beneficial gratitude was. As a result, I probably robbed myself of so much joy. It may've also affected my healing. I even bought a pretty journal to jot down my blessings, but it was hard for me to slow down enough to do so.

In hindsight, even though not everything in my life met my high degree of expectations, I realize I had numerous things for which to be thankful! Now, it is one of the quickest ways for me to get in a better mood. What are some things for which you are grateful?

6. *Laugh!* – When was the last time you had a good laugh?! The benefits of laughter are vast. Gendry (n.d.) says laughter is beneficial for body, mind, and spirit. Laughter is good for our circulatory, nervous, respiratory, and immune systems. Some medical applications are to treat diabetes, Alzheimer's, Parkinson's, mental health, substance abuse, fertility, and aids in prevention of and recovery from, cancer.

During a severe part of dealing with bad health conditions, I would watch Duck Dynasty's crazy antics to give me that pick me up. I know they can be somewhat controversial, but you've got to admit, Si is a riot! However, if that's not your cup of tea, try some of Gendry's (n.d.) laughter therapy. Gendry (n.d.) has laughter down to a science and lists several ways to implement what he calls laughter therapy and "kick-start your laughter" … which includes laughter warm-ups, gradient laughter, laughter sneeze, and singing laughter.

7. *Put the brakes on profanity* – Personally, I've never felt comfortable using curse words, so I replaced them with words like "poop," or the more endearing "poopie," when unpleasant things happened. I would even do it if I was upset or disappointed at myself. Ever since I've been practicing cultivating a more positive state of mind, I realized that even these words, or probably more so the attitude behind them, made me feel down, like a sludgy heaviness.

It may not seem like much, but little doses of negativity can add up. Try being understanding. Or, use one of the strategies listed here to get you into a better mindset.

8. *Knowing God loves me!* – This is the one that made the biggest difference for me. I had to realize that God loves me without conditions and independent of my performance. I have to remind myself constantly that no matter what, even if I fail, God loves me. He has plans to prosper me and looks out for me (Jer. 29:11; Ps. 37:23-25). I just have to trust Him and be open to receiving His Love & blessings. :-)

9. *Apply it!* – When have you had enjoyable moments in life? What helps you to be happy? Many of us have probably heard of some, if not all the strategies I outlined. Or you may have additional things that work for you and fit your lifestyle. Not only that but doctors, studies about the effects of stress, the benefits of positivity, even our bodies tell us that we are better off applying these and similar strategies.

Yes, we may have a full calendar but aren't you, your dreams, and goals worth it? You'll be more positive, easier to get along with, more productive, creative, and most of all, you will actually be living and enjoying your life.

10. *Hire a life coach* – Do you need someone who will encourage, listen, challenge you, and most of all, keep you accountable all within a judgement-free zone? If you are ready to change and be propelled to the next level, you may want to hire a life coach. Research shows that having a coach will help you reach your goals quicker. Of course, the effects depend on the effort you put forth. Also, make sure there is a good-fit between you and your coach.

There are plenty more strategies to help us enjoy our lives! These are some of the main ones that worked for me. It took some time and effort to implement them and make them a part of my life. I hope the ones I've included in this chapter help you live a more satisfying life wherever this finds you. Start with one, or a couple if you feel adventurous. Like any other habit we try to adopt, we may fall off the rails at times. Just remember to be kind to yourself and try again. If I could do this, you can, too.

Now, ready, set, go live and enjoy your life! :-)

References

Achor, S. (2012). Positive intelligence. *Harvard Business Review*. Retrieved from
    https://hbr.org/2012/01/positive-intelligence
Gendry, S. (n.d.). benefits of laughter. *Laughter Online University*. Retrieved from
    http://www.laughteronlineuniversity.com/category/science/
Moore, M. (2010, January 30). How coaching works: Appreciative Inquiry. *Psychology Today*.
    Retrieved from https://www.psychologytoday.com/blog/life-changes/201001/how-
    coaching-works-appreciative-inquiry
Relaxation techniques: Breath control helps quell errant stress response. (2016, March 18).
    Harvard Health Publications. Harvard Medical School. Retrieved from
    http://www.health.harvard.edu/mind-and-mood/relaxation-techniques-breath-control-
    helps-quell-errant-stress-response

About Violet

Violet Detre helps her clients reignite their passion for success and for life. As a gifted student in her formative years, she was primed to reach the pinnacles of success, but was stunted by unfortunate circumstances and life's challenges. Through it all, she learned that it was possible to not just survive the day-to-day but to achieve personal fulfillment.

Violet's life coaching business is centered on her belief that one can reach their goals at a faster rate and with more ease by enjoying one's life in this moment. As a life coach, Violet's passion is to help professionals who feel run down or burnt out regain zeal and enjoyment in their careers and lives.

Violet holds a bachelor's degree in Education and Life Coaching from Liberty University (*summa cum laude*). At present, she is completing her Graduate Certificate in Professional and Executive Coaching and is on the ICF certification track. As a member of the American Association of Christian Counselors, she heeds to her call: assisting people to be the best version of themselves.

Violet was born and raised in Laredo, Texas. Currently, she lives with her husband of 20 years in Florida.

CHAPTER 21

A LIFE TO LIVE – NOT TO DIE

BY GRACE MARTINS

So many talks, so many walks,
So many cheers, so many tears,
So many laughs, so many hugs.

Neither our body nor our heart will dominate us. Our mind can control both. An effort toward harmony between mind, heart, spirit, and body would overturn difficult situations. Making intelligent decisions will only make us wiser.

Choosing quality rather than quantity, reinforcing life with kind words would transform a way of living to a simple and extraordinary way to enjoy present moments.

We do our hair, we do our nails,
We love to buy shoes, we love to buy purses,
We hardly talk, we hardly walk,
We forget to pray, we forget our faith.

We feed our body and dress it too, but we forget to feed our brain, our heart, and our spirit; rather, we torment our soul and mind with worries about the past of yesterday. Focus on today, understanding that we can't bring yesterday back, and whatever happened yesterday are signs of the past. We cannot change or reverse the past, but only change our attitude or perspective toward future misfortunes.

About tomorrow, it is not here yet, and "if" tomorrow arrives and we wake-up, we will have "today." So why worry? Why not? "Feeling so beautiful alive."

All those unnecessary worries are robbing our present time and with it, our creativity to be successful in life:

❖ Embracing life as it comes as a cheerleader, appreciating the cheer up there in the air.

❖ Listening to others could help to clarify that life is not perfect, and interruptions occur like in nature, chiefly in tropical climates and not one can prevent it.

❖ If our disappointment or pain from the loss of a boyfriend or something else is the reason to stop us from living, we must say we have got everything wrong.

❖ Because life is full of everything and not being thankful for all those past mistakes, we would not have learned to cope with internal waves.

❖ Observing trees, birds, and running water, all of them capture our attention in different ways, we just have to observe what life has to offer, not so far from us.

Like the sea waves retreat after crashing on shore, leaving uncovered, right there in front of our eyes on the sand, all types of things. A natural canvas with lines drawn by water painted full of new surprises to amaze us. If we just take a little time to think, we can compare canvases with a Chinese picture, beautiful and spacious –allowing your mind to wander.

Open our eyes to uncover the possibilities that life has to offer daily, which can result in a clear mind.

If we are questioning ourselves and start to concentrate more on what is important in life, taking note of our individual habits in general. Also, the way we perceive things can be changed if we are not satisfied with ourselves. It is not necessary to overdo everything in one day, but taking steps to leave the "human drama" and focus on few simple steps. We must concentrate not on what others are recommending; rather, listen and observe and chose the new paths. Retraining the mind to listen, breathe, and read Nobel books by foreign authors. It's not only to enrich our vocabulary, but also our life, with knowledge about other countries customs, and traditions—allowing us to understand other traditions. It can untangle or unwrap our daily boring routines, and who knows what else we can discover of what we are capable.

The sun in the sky,
Reflecting on all those eyes.
The sun in the sky,
That keeps so many warm,
Transforming many lives,
The sun in the sky keeps us aware, and our faith alive.

If our heart is wounded, help it to restore the meaning of life. Not everyone believes in God, but it could be the reason for feeling disconnected or overwhelmed with so much media to absorb, but it doesn't have to be this way. We are free to choose what we allow ourselves to watch or listen.

We do have a life to live not to die.

Daily we hear, "She said or he said this or that." If we remember our roots and where we stand tall in life like a tree, we understand it doesn't matter, we do have the power of preventing negative feelings – not easy but possible; it is up to us, not to them. Loving who we are will give us the confidence to visualize new horizons and challenges. It would and it could impress or amaze ourselves and of course those that we call friends.

Getting up and trying again and again, we will eventually reach what we are striving to accomplish. As an individual we are different and unique absorbing and learning new tasks that can take time. It is okay to feel alone, but feeling lonely is not the right of way of living and feeling beautiful and alive.

So get out there—find all the wonders to a beautiful life!

Leave those fears at home or throw them out – have a few bruises and feel the love and pain of getting up again; it is a deep 'dearie' in everyone that fails not once and not twice, but it doesn't matter the count, because that is part of being alive and keep in mind we have . . . "a life to live not to die."

About Grace

You may ask who is Grace Martins? For many around, they know her as a strong character that never gives up, never receives 'no' as an answer, and has a strong passion for living a beautiful life. She has always been a strong being from the beginning.

She grew up in South America on a farm and a very religious and strict boarding school, where imagination and creativity was hidden from most individuals. She later found love that brought her to the United States. She found herself here adopting a new culture and a new way of life.

As time passed, she had three beautiful daughters. Raising them, she not only allowed them to become free and independent but, also taught them that life has so much more to offer if you just open your eyes and see the beauty around them. Meantime their way of life also taught her that life is not all bills and stress, but rather, together they learned that joy exists even in the hardest of times.

Now with her children grown up and free time on her hands, she finds herself unable to contain all those wonders in this world to herself. She knew she had not only a passion, but perhaps a talent to express life, thoughts, images, and wonders in this world in short stories as she continues to polish the English language.

CHAPTER 22

MENTAL TENACITY

BY DON LAWRENCE

I see only my objective – the obstacles must give way.
~ Napoleon Bonaparte

In the 1984 movie, *Mask*, the leading character, Rocky Dennis, shared a self-written poem:

These things are good, the rain on my tongue, the sun in my face.
These things are a drag, the rain on my tongue, the sun in my face.

And such is the life of the entrepreneur.

We who have been given the gift of an entrepreneurial spirit know all too well that it is a love/hate relationship. A relationship with highs so high that it seems you can touch the clouds. And yet there are times when the lows are so low you just want to quit, crawl into a hole and hope to find your sanity again. It is easy to go through the fun times, and there are many. The trick is how does one get through the difficult times and find the courage to stay the course.

Ever since I was a small boy, I was drawn to creating income from nothing. Cutting grass for my church and its parsonage, hauling groceries at the local A&P store, building bikes from old junk parts I found in the county landfill and then selling the bikes to my friends from my backyard – this was my introduction to entrepreneurship. Growing up, I tried working "real jobs" but I always found myself attracted to the freedom of mastering my own destiny. I started my first contracting business at nineteen years old and I bought my first investment property that same year. I have been self-employed ever since. Looking back was never an option.

Tenacity: The Entrepreneur's Essential Ingredient

If I were asked the question, "What word would you use to attribute your success as an entrepreneur?" I would answer with, "Tenacity." Without tenacity, one might as well hang up his dreams of success as an entrepreneur.

What is tenacity anyway? Tenacity's root word is "tenacious." Merriam-Webster's Dictionary's defines tenacity as "persistent in maintaining, adhering to, or seeking something valued or desired." Additionally, Merriam-Webster's Dictionary uses words such as "courage, mettle, spirit" and "resolution" to describe tenacity.

Every business comes with its own set of challenges. Entrepreneurship can be a lonely place and it will require tenacity to forge ahead. You must know deep inside yourself that you have what it takes to get through the rough spots to stay in the game.

As a real estate investor, developer, and contractor, I know all too well what it feels like to lose hundreds of thousands of dollars in an instant when the market crashes. I know what it feels like to start a new venture, investing everything you have in an idea you believe in, and after two years of hard work it is not successful. But I also know that success does not find itself, you find it. Entrepreneurship is not without its challenges. However, it comes with many rewards. As for me, I know firsthand, it's worth it.

For thirty-seven years, I have owned and operated my own businesses and I have concluded that the most important quality a person must possess is tenacity to succeed as a business owner. I have heard it said that a wise man learns from his own mistakes, but a wiser man learns from the mistakes of others.

I'd like to share with you the lessons I've discovered in my journey of becoming a tenacious entrepreneur, so that you may have the opportunity to learn from and apply them to your own business path.

1. <u>Are you in the right business?</u>

We entrepreneurs can be a bit scatterbrained at times. Most creative people are. We are good at many things and it is like herding cats just trying to figure out what path we should take. You have your skills but the real challenge is finding your gifts and then moving in that direction. When I started contracting and real estate, I didn't focus on the fact that I love to communicate and coach people. I wasted precious time going left when I should have gone right. I have discovered that my passion is writing, speaking and coaching and I am now moving in that direction. I manage my own real estate and construction businesses not because I love it but because I am good at it. My real gift is the "gift of gab" and now I am living my passion. Don't do as I did; find your passion before you launch your business.

Guiding Principle:

Before embarking on your entrepreneurial endeavor, sit down and ask yourself, what gives me real joy and contentment? What am I passionate about and how may I turn this into an income-producing conduit? Doing what you love will give you the strength to tenaciously stay the course through the tough times. Someone once said do what you love and you will never work a day in your life. Work your passion and live your dream. You will then enjoy a rewarding entrepreneurial journey.

2. <u>Do you know your why?</u>

Knowing why you want to be in business for yourself will provide the foundation for tenacity. To weather the storms that will most certainly come, you must know why you would place yourself in this predicament in the first place. When hard times arrive, knowing your why is essential to your success. For me, I do it because I want to help others find their 'sweet spot' in business and in life. Few things give me more pleasure than writing a book or the energy I receive when speaking on stage. I do it for personal freedom and I do it to have, be and do whatever I want. I live life on my terms.

Guiding Principle:

Whether you are a start-up company or if you are thinking about starting one, I encourage you to revisit your why. Your why needs to be so important to you that nothing will deter you from success. To achieve mental tenacity, your why must and will be the reason for pushing yourself through the inevitable obstacles. If you desire something deeply enough, then you will have it. Why do you do it? Make your list, own it, and make it count. It must come from deep within your soul, and it must be a part of your inner core being to matter in the hard times.

3. <u>Do you fight or flight?</u>

At the beginning of our existence, we humans lived in caves and our brains were wired to know when to fight off a predator or run like heck to save ourselves from danger or even death. As an entrepreneur, there may come a time when you will be faced with the prospect of the death of your business. Through no fault of your own, a partner made a stupid decision and costs the company money it did not have to lose. Perhaps the market crashed, you were caught up in the vacuum and now, you are being consumed. Regardless of the cause, when the time comes you must do something about it. It is time to stand your ground and fight with everything you have in you. Fleeing is not an option. Tenacity is the only way.

Guiding Principle:

You are a creative person; use your creativity as a weapon. You did not get this far by being timid, scared and unimaginative. Begin to paint pictures of the answers in your mind. When things seem hopeless, you must adopt an "I-will-not-quit" attitude. We become what we think about. If you are thinking defeat, then you are already defeated. Talk to other entrepreneurs for advice. Many times, an idea will flow from them that will rescue you from the challenges you are facing. Learn from your mistakes and apply those lessons to your resolve. The great orator and former Prime Minister of Britain, Winston Churchill, said, "If you're going through hell, keep going." You need to reach for that tenacious place within yourself to persevere.

4. <u>Are you your own safety net?</u>

It is not always easy for people to accept responsibility for their actions. So many individuals are looking for a bail-out. When the housing crises occurred a few years ago, the government and the American taxpayers bailed out the big banks and the auto industry. Whether that was a good thing or not, I do not know. Perhaps time will tell. But one thing is for sure, as an entrepreneur you must stand on your own two feet because no one is going to bail you out. You must expect the unexpected and be ready for the inevitable. Things will go wrong and you will have to be tenacious in your resolve.

Guiding Principle:

If you are like most entrepreneurs you are always undercapitalized. So, you have to rely on creative ideas and other means to survive. Coming up with ideas to weather the storm before the storm hits is always a good idea. Having a "Plan B" is paramount.

Before investing in a property, I want to know if I can live with the downside. If the downside isn't significant, I most likely will buy the property. I have lost money on investment properties, but I hold on to the memories of the successful ones. You must always leave yourself room to land on your feet. Calculate the risk before diving in head first. The responsibility is yours and yours alone to protect yourself from failure.

However, when failure happens as it sometimes will, you must be tenacious in finding a solution. I know of no better approach to solve any challenge but through being tenacious and constantly pursuing a positive result.

5. <u>Can you do one more rep?</u>

In the early eighties, I owned two health clubs that catered to the hardcore body builder. In 1989, the health club sponsored a contestant for the "Mr. Maryland Body Building Contest" and he won first place. I would watch Don work out and it always amazed me how he could pack on such large muscle mass on his 5'6" frame. I asked him what his secret was. He told me that you need to load the bar with the maximum amount of weight you can handle for ten repetitions and then force yourself to do one more rep.

While working out in my home gym yesterday morning, feeling tired and fatigued, I reached for a dumbbell to do the last set of exercises. Immediately, I put the weight down and said to myself, "Nope! I'm done. I'm too tired." And, at that very moment, I saw Don in my mind's eye saying to me, "One more rep!" I found the courage and strength to finish my workout and the feeling of accomplishment was exhilarating.

Guiding Principle:

The same lessons may be learned in our businesses and in life. When you absolutely feel you cannot take one more hit or go one more round, you have to draw from a place that keeps you going. You need to say to yourself, "Just one more rep! I'm going to give it one more try. I'm going to make this thing happen if it kills me. I will not quit!" Although the urge to give up may present itself, be tenacious and do one more rep.

My hope is that the lessons I have shared above will serve as the GPS for your journey as an entrepreneur. I trust you will find that your destination is a successful one and that the lessons learned here will aid you in your endeavors.

If you can answer the following questions:

- *Are you in the right business?*
- *Do you know your why?*
- *Do you fight or flight?*
- *Are you your own safety net?*
- *Can you do one more rep?*

. . . then all that remains is the tenacious pursuit of a worthy goal as a successful entrepreneur!

About Don

Don Lawrence, an accomplished entrepreneur since the age of 19 and an over-the-top husband, father and grandfather, lives in Freeland, Maryland where he and his wife enjoy their 26-acre farm. He is the proud father of an adult son and an adult daughter who have blessed him with a daughter-in-law, a son-in-law, a 10-year-old grandson and an 8-month-old granddaughter.

Professionally, Don is known mostly for his contracting business and real estate development ventures. In addition, Don provides mentoring as a real estate coach and enjoys motivational public speaking.

With Don's focus on health, he is a certified fitness trainer and a recreational body builder.

Don is an experienced lead guitar player and has served as a praise and worship leader for years within the church.

While a survivor of ulcerative colitis, Don is positioned to share his story of facing only two weeks to live and how he decided instantly to live a full life. Don is known within his professional and personal circle for his passion to share his life's lessons in an effort to assist others in making significant positive changes to their own life.

With a focus on getting his messages to the thousands, it is Don's desire to broaden his audience via his upcoming book entitled, *Tragedy's Gifts*.

You can connect with Don at:
- contact@donlawrencejr.com

CHAPTER 23

GET UNSTUCK ... THEN GO!

BY SHERRYL MELLOTT McGUIRE

What's holding you back? What's getting in the way of you being the best YOU ever? We all have a life story with beauty marks and warts. Things happen in early childhood, high school, first job, marriage, children … you name it! It's called LIFE, and no one is immune. Things can get stuck in our psyche and our body to give us continuous grief and distract us from our true calling. This can get in the way of a healthy professional and personal life. They do not make up a psychological disorder. You don't have a mental illness or permanent emotional dysfunction. But you are gridlocked. Immobilized. Shipwrecked on your own island. The good news … you can mobilize again … after all, it is YOUR island.

Tom's story illustrates how we can mobilize to change old habits. It is quite similar to many other clients' stories.

By all outward measures, Tom was a successful dentist. But it hadn't always been easy for him in high school. He graduated with a B-minus; nevertheless, his parents clearly impressed upon him that he was college-bound. He had trouble communicating, got into fights, and was generally unhappy until he joined a group of guys going to college. Things turned around. He knew he needed to work by himself, because he didn't really understand how to work with others very well or deal with conflict or make changes. In college and dental school, he graduated with a B average. Two years later, he bought a dentistry practice and did well for several years.

Soon the facility looked dated. Everything needed to be redone and changed: remodeling, marketing, redesigning service packages, increasing prices, buying furniture and redoing processes and systems. It was overwhelming! He languished for four years doing nothing. Profits decreased. His motivation was in the tank. He hated dealing with employee issues, avoiding them till they blew up. He did not want to re-invest more money in the business. He was fraught with procrastination, poor attitude, lack of energy/enthusiasm. In fact, he was burned out. It just wasn't as interesting as it used to be. He needed the accomplishment of becoming a successful dentist more than he enjoyed the actual work of dentistry. He sold the practice. He didn't know what he wanted to do.

He enjoyed making money; he developed a real estate investment business that did well. But his burning desire was to have time with his male friends, and a couple of older uncles whom he felt especially close to as a child. His two sons were in college, his wife was a busy sales manager, traveling over half the time. He was on his own a lot. Friends were his primary focus. Then his best friend suddenly died, followed by the death of two uncles and his mother; he was sad and full of grief. Shortly thereafter, his other best friend also died early. Most of the people who meant so much to him were gone. Anxiety and mild depression took root in his everyday life. He felt lonely and alone; he didn't know what was happening to him. He was emotionally bankrupt without understanding why or what to do.

Tom was slowly able to identify the childhood obstacles that had so unsettled him. He had puzzled over why he couldn't work well with others. His wife had been frustrated as to why he walled off his family emotionally and placed an over-importance on friends. He was lost. His understanding developed as to the anxiety, grief, mania, obsession, compulsion, and delusion that had taken over his life during the grieving process.

Working with a coach, a plan was begun. First, he started by re-connecting with his family, who were still there for him. They let him know they cared for his well-being; he began to express his love and devotion to them, which involved new beliefs and behaviors on his part. He began talking about what happened to him, and how he derailed.

He did not have a psychological disorder; it was a development delay from early childhood neglect. With the coach, he devised steps to learn relational skills, along with an even fuller understanding of development delays and what to do about them.

Tom began to understand the walls he had constructed and why he felt compelled to hide behind them. He learned about emotions and how they helped him to identify what he needed and wanted. Grief is a normal, healthy emotion that we all can learn to manage; it doesn't have to overwhelm us. Tom began to express this and other feelings especially with his wife and family. He worked at adding feeling words to match what he was experiencing. He actively sought out and perceived his family as his core group to belong. He learned to love deeply, feel other emotions more clearly, and discuss what he wanted in life and in work. He could relate to all types of friends better without expecting them to be his primary connection. He went back to work. His business slowly began to improve. He developed the emotional intelligence he needed. Life became rewarding, peaceful and meaningful. There was an internal calmness he had never known.

What are the symptoms of being stuck? ... being held back emotionally? ... procrastination, excessive fears, anxiety, worry, depression, inertia. The glass is half empty. Being frozen or numb. Negative self-talk, and anger for no apparent reason. Frequently there is poor self-esteem, feelings of inadequacy, and perhaps excessive passiveness, or the opposite, excessive mania. You may have a sense you don't belong anywhere and have a frequent need for validation. You may put others first to the point of ignoring your own basic self-needs or you may be dismissing your closest loved ones. There can also be anxiety, delusion, obsession, compulsion, irrational thought, unavailable feelings, and self-destructive behaviors (alcohol, drugs, sex, food, gambling, excess exercise, workaholism). Many people have these things occur during stress, grief, and tough circumstances, but they do not stick for long. Under typical circumstances, they are not pervasive. Tom's symptoms lasted 43 years before he knew they were unhealthy. He learned quickly and recovered.

We are imperfect, flawed human beings. This frequently shows in our professional and business choices and behaviors. The more unaware and unconscious we are of how these affect us and others, the greater the impact they have. Why? Because we are operating from our subconscious habits. We may not even know where these barriers came from, especially if something happened during early childhood. So many times, the feelings of inadequacy, not fitting in, emptiness, lack of confidence, fear, anxiety, depression, or pervasive "downer" states, can come from a time we don't even remember. Or, we might remember, but when we are young and vulnerable, these often have a HUGE imprint on us. Beliefs greatly influence habits. Pay attention to your "programmed" habits to better understand what you are doing. Our habits control our lives – when aware of them, we can change them with our conscious mind. We can think and behave our way into the person we want to be.

If you are stuck / feeling empty you can heal yourself, but not entirely by yourself. You need other resources. You cannot know what you want if you are trapped in old internal conflicts. You can be the lead architect to envision a plan, execute the plan and take the steps you want/need to take. Use a good coach who understands developmental delays (not just psychological disorders) and has knowledge of emotional issues. This person also needs to understand what occurs to adults when they are derailed as children. A good coach has a wealth of methods to suggest for overcoming delays. The coach is your basic helper and they will refer you to other specialists as needed. A coach can provide ideas, identify the importance of certain steps, monitor progress, discuss the meaningfulness of your improvements, and help you navigate difficult situations. Plus, they will help you celebrate accomplishments!

What are the Steps for Overcoming Obstacles and Getting Mobilized?

1. <u>We are what we believe.</u>

   You need to gather the courage to address the issue(s) getting in your way. Harness your brain power by using the 5% of the brain's pre-frontal cortex, the seat of consciousness. Life's wounds often create barriers that immobilize us in the old 95% programming. Dr. Bruce Lipton,[1] a biologist, says "change your perception (mind) and your body changes." Lipton explains the subconscious mind, which generates 95% of our habits. It is mostly formed by the time we are seven years old. Today, most of us live from this 95%. What we unconsciously absorbed from those experiences and people around us make up the vast majority of our beliefs today. And now 30, 40,

---

[1] Catharina Roland, *Awake in the Dream*. Retrieved from: ttps://www.brucelipton.com/store/awake-the-dream-dvd

or 50+ years later, those situations are still embedded in our brain and habits.

Previously the 95% beliefs may have served to protect us. As we grow, they work against us—walling off new ideas, new information, certain people, and new ways of living. Living in the 95% blocks us from reinventing ourselves. When we excessively worry about a new challenge, struggle to prepare for the promotion, wring our hands with problems, become afraid of pursuing a new business, or become obsessed with any change, we are STUCK in the 95%. Our 5% conscious mind struggles against the subconscious programming. Sometimes these negative beliefs foster destructive habits like addictions. If these are severe, they can affect us for decades, or even kill us.

We can be mostly successful, somewhat happy, partially fulfilled, yet there is this nagging feeling we are not good enough. This may translate to an awareness that we didn't get enough emotional support—attention, affection or sense of empowerment. Or worse, some deal with overt abuse they struggled with their whole lives... feeling as though they just barely survive.

This can change, and often more easily than you might think. The conscious mind in the pre-frontal cortex involves: living in the NOW, creativity, planning, reinventing ourselves, making decisions and solving problems. You hold the key to switching your brain from 95% to 5%. It takes intentional, conscious effort. You are what you think, so think in a different way; become the creator of your life.

2. <u>Choose a psychologically-trained life or educational coach.</u>

What you need from a coach: knowledge, skills, someone who resonates with you, availability, positive approach to growth and the ability to celebrate the small wins along the journey.

3. <u>Intentionally engage with others who are good for you and who will help you transform yourself.</u>

Find a mastermind group or gather a group of friends to listen to you. They will often give you effective feedback. Explain what, how and why you want to do things. Stop thinking you have to know or do it all; no one does it all. Remind yourself you are not stuck; experiment with you!

4. Survey the area(s) of life that hold you back, where old beliefs block you from fully living and stepping into your new world.

With your coach, describe these, look at how you acquired them, re-think whether they work for you today. Discuss how and with what you will replace them.

5. Take specific steps for re-imaging yourself as the entrepreneur, professional, business person or individual you desire to be.

Identify the characteristics you are working to incorporate. What knowledge do you have for this new venture? What resources can you use when you do not know what to do? What are the next steps to get there?

6. Believe in yourself.

Work at a positive self-concept. Love yourself (warts and all), knowing that your body, mind, and spirit is continuously evolving. We are different people at age 60 than at age 30.

7. Seek your highest self – trust your intuition and divine guidance – it is the "best" you.

Start a new daily habit: consult with God, Higher Power, Spirit, Jesus or with whomever you relate.

8. Choose to live intentionally, with the 5% conscious mind.

Intentionally choose the direction of many aspects of your life. You no longer need to be unconsciously "pre-programmed."

9. Clarify your requirements.

What other resources do you need to accomplish your business or professional goals, e.g., strategist, accountant, writer, etc. You can't do it all.

10. <u>Develop a written plan for breaking out of the old programmed habits.</u>

Eliminate specific issues holding you back from accessing the 5% conscious brain. Act on your current thinking and feeling.

a. With the coach, discuss the details of these preprogrammed habits in your life that keep you stuck.

b. Express the emotions and feelings that go along with these old habits. Institute a plan for how to deal with the emotions and feelings more effectively.

c. Imagine, think and plan how you want YOU to manifest in the workplace or your personal life.

d. Identify what you will do and outline how you want to do it.

e. Discuss what you want to do with knowledgeable people who will give you feedback.

f. Start implementing the most practical step first. Then choose the second step, third step, etc.

g. Continuously talk about the new you with your coach, and others (best friend, spouse, sister, colleague, etc.) Be sure they understand what you are saying, and they serve an up-lifting, positive force in your life.

h. Identify other people who can help you in business or professional development: financial planner, business strategist, web developer or trainer.

i. Establish objectives and steps to grow in your confidence and emotional intelligence.

j. Implement and evaluate your plan with your coach, discussing your progress along the way.

k. Celebrate each and every win – small and large!

When you commit to mobilizing your career or life now, it will be a **"Ready, Set, Go!"** frame of mind. Nothing will hold you back; you are no longer trapped in internal conflicts. It is all so worth it!

Live healthy, calm and re-charged for life!

About Sherryl

Sherryl Mellott McGuire's life-long passion and reward has been helping people grow. She came from a family of entrepreneurs who strongly believed in helping people develop their full potential. Sherryl has followed those footsteps, working in human resources since 1976, in many different roles with public and private organizations. She founded and served as the Director of a nonprofit organization. In 1981, she began working as a career coach and counselor. Then in 1989 she became a Consultant in the rehabilitation management field, traveling throughout the US and its territories. She developed a four-week rigorous program for Executive Leaders in Rehabilitation. This program exemplified Sherryl's approach to leadership. It is people oriented and strategic as a "best practice" for maximizing service organizations' credibility and customer/client orientation.

Sherryl consults in strategic planning, team building, conflict resolution, customer service, executive/management development and stress management. Her clients range from professional practitioners—insurance, veterinary services, dentistry, human resources, hospitals and health organizations. Her client organizations include small- and medium-sized businesses and public organizations.

Sherryl graduated with a B.S. and M.S. in Applied Behavioral Studies from Oklahoma State University and a Ph.D. from the University of Oklahoma in Adult/Higher Education (emphasis Organization/Employee Development and Change). She is a writer, speaker, career coach/counselor and university professor. Her expertise is based on many hours of study and practice in psychology (both with individuals and organizations), including personnel training and development. For 32 years she has taught online and in-country classes in psychology and human resource management for the University of Oklahoma's worldwide Masters' Degree Program in Human Relations.

Coaching clients is her most interesting and challenging work – particularly with leaders, managers and professionals. It often involves helping individuals reinvent themselves as well as apply their "new" self in a different business or professional challenge. She has written numerous articles and papers in the area of human resource leadership and management, including career coaching. She has been a speaker for multiple organizations and trade associations in the field of vocational rehabilitation, economic development and government.

You can reach Sherryl at:
- Email: shermcg@gmail.com
- Website: www.sherrylmcguirecoach.com
- Facebook: www.facebook.com/CoachingWritingSpeaking/

CHAPTER 24

SIX STRATEGIES TO BUILD AND GROW AN UNSHAKEABLE BUSINESS, EVEN WITHOUT THE INTERNET

BY PATRICK RAHN

Are you feeling overwhelmed with all the new technology and tools that exist in today's market? Is it because you don't know where to start the digitalization of your business, not to mention the pressure you feel as you watch young tech businesses take off? Well, you do not have to, and do you know why?

Because the Internet, Social Media, Search Engine Optimization, Pay-Per-Click and all that online tech stuff are just tools. If you know how to use those tools without knowing why and when to use them, you're set to fail.

It is like your knowing how to use a hammer and a saw, and as a result think that you can build your dream house. However, without a blueprint, a framework or a set of rules for how and when to use each tool – in short without a plan – your dream house build is set to fail. It's not about the fancy new tools, it's about proven strategies.

First, I started an offline business and tried to sell fun sports articles, but I failed miserably. I then switched to selling stuff online, learning all about the online marketing tools, but failed a second time. This caused me frustration as I wondered why my beautiful dream house kept on collapsing every time.

Well, I later found out why I thought I was the smartest guy in town. I did seek advice and had a plan, but I was under the impression that the fundamentals did not work anymore. I thought that I had to reinvent the wheel because I had knowledge on all the new technology. This caused me to think that with the changing times, what worked 20 to 30 years ago did not work anymore; that was my biggest mistake.

I was on the verge of giving up my dreams. But then I decided to give it one last try. To be honest, I gave myself this last try a little more than once. I committed myself to building strong fundamental business foundations that had been proven to be useful by history over and over again. I studied business and business psychology and found a common theme in every successful business (including the Walmarts, Coca-Colas, Apples and Teslas of the world). I was committed to set up my foundation on principles and strategies that are proven to be successful, and after that I could test my creativity and play with ideas.

And to my astonishment, it worked better than I had anticipated. That is why I have decided to share the six primary and most crucial strategies that you can use to build an unshakeable business foundation. I learned the hard way, but you do not have to.

1. Own Your Market/Niche

Most business owners focus on finding a niche in the market and set up their business in it. Well, in truth, that is what I did. That, however just gets you a spot in an already dominated market, making you just another business person offering the same product or service. And with just that, there is no way you can outperform the company that dominates your market. That means that if your product or service is not the first or at least 10x better than the others in your market or niche, then you are running a business that is destined to fail.

You would be much better off to create your own sub-niche in the already existing niche. Find something for your business to be the first to provide in the already existing products or services offered within your market. That right there is a foundation that will make your business undoubtedly unshakeable.

Take for instance the iPhone. Before the 29th of June 2007, Apple did not have a product for the mobile phone market. Back then, cell phone companies like Nokia, Blackberry, Motorola, and Sony Ericson were the most popular mobile companies. Apple could have made a mobile that imitated the rest and stayed at the back of the sales line with dormant sales. But they had a better plan, to create their kind of smartphone; the iPhone. It was a revolution in the smartphone industry because there was none like it.

By 2015, Apple had recorded the biggest annual profit in corporate history. Now every mobile phone company had to make their smartphones that tried to be like the iPhone – just to stay relevant. That is what creating your niche or market can do for your business.

Ask yourself: How can I position my product or business so that it becomes its own unique, hot sub-niche?

2. The Magical Power – An Upsell-Downsell Funnel

I think a lot of business owners underestimate the power of sales funnels especially upsell-downsell funnels. The upsell-downsell funnels are where the real money is if you use them well.

Business owners that do not have these sales funnels yet, probably do not quite understand how they work. To them, it is still a secret.

In case you do not know what an upsell is, an upsell entails a simple question, "would like to purchase another service or product to go with the one you have already purchased?" The question is, however, strategically structured and placed at a position where the buyer sees more value in the acquisition.

A perfect example would be McDonald's. A customer bought a simple meal of medium-sized French fries for $1.79. Then the upsell is induced by the simple question, "Would you like a Coke to go with your fries?" Note that not all customers will buy the extra coke for $1.49, but for the many that will, McDonald's on average added an extra 20-30% increase to their profit.

What would an extra 20-30% increase in profits mean to you, your business and your family?

As for the downsell funnel, it entails a simple offer. Have you ever walked into a shop, for instance a shoe store, looking for limited edition sneakers, then you realize that they are way above your price range? But then the seller offers you the previous edition for say, half the price. Well, it is not what you came for, but the deal is too good to refuse. And in the end, it's a win-win.

Remember that it is your moral obligation to give your customer the best possible outcome of what they desire. This will also culminate in sales and profits for your business.

How can you add more value for your customers?

3. Focus On the Backend

Have you ever wondered why some business owners can spend more on marketing and PR than you? Well, the answer is simple, it is because they are aware of the secret of focusing on the backend. The backend gives your business the exposure it needs to beat the competition.

Most businesses focus on making a profit on the first sale. You might be thinking, "Patrick, how can I survive without making a profit on the first sale?" Well, you need to focus on your Lifetime Customer Value (LCV). The LCV is the worst case average value of a 30-day, 90-day or even a one-to-two-year customer repurchase cycle (this depends on your product or service and your cash flow abilities).

Let us say the average new customer brings to your store an average profit of $50 on the first sale. He or she repurchases three more times a year with an average reorder amount of $200, and with a gross profit of $75 for every repurchase. Now, with the average customer lasting two years, every new customer is worth $500. Allow me to do the math for you: $50 + (3 repurchases x $75 x 2 years) = $500.

Because you now know that your customer is worth $500 all through his or her lifetime, you can confidently decide to outspend your competitors in acquiring customers. You can spend for instance $50, when your competitor is only willing to spend $20 to $30, because they think they need to make profit upfront, considering they are not aware of their LCV. That means you can get more customers into your business than your competitors.

Remember, the business that is willing and can afford to spend more to acquire a customer wins.

What's your LCV?

4. S.T.M. = Growth Maximizer

This strategy is one of my favorite, most effective and fun ways you can use to build firm ground to establish your business and build a brand. It is an approach that saves you the frustrations of having to travel for miles just to try and convince a client to buy your product or service – a client who might end up saying "no". It can save you frustrations of having to hire a sales team even though your business cannot afford it yet, or the frustrations of spending loads of time describing your product or service over and over again, rather than selling it. S.T.M. changed all that for my business, now I only spend 5% of my time selling, and the rest I can spend on serving my clients.

S.T.M. stands for Sale-To-Many, and it involves the use of seminars, webinars, info days, conferences and even books and magazines to sell your product or service. All these are avenues that enable you to get in front of your target market on a large-scale platform. Plus, it is the best way for authoritative selling, where you get to describe your product or service and its benefits to a wide range of consumers at one time. This is one instance in which interested buyers call you instead of you going after them – not to mention the exposure your business will get. And with this approach, every call you receive has more potential for a sale given that you already have the buyer's interest – unlike the sale-to-one approach.

A perfect example of a successful S.T.M. forum is the TED Talk. TED is the gold standard for any conference. And for the businesses that are presented on that stage, well, it goes without saying that they are tops in their markets.

What STM approach can you use (webinar, seminar, infodays, books etc.) to sell your product or service?

5. Master the Art of Follow-Up

This is one of the most common and perhaps my biggest mistake made at the beginning of my career in business. This cost me dearly – hundreds of thousands of dollars and emotional distress. It is all about pitching the right message to the right client at the right time. The message and the client part are the "easy" parts. The right time, however, is not easily known. So how do you deal with that predicament? Well, it is rather simple, be there consistently until the right time unveils itself, by regularly following up.

You know the drill when you do your pitch to a potential client, and then they tell that they are not ready to buy yet due to reason 'A' or 'B'. But by the time they are willing, your competition had them already boxed in. Mastering the Art of Follow-up makes you own the client's loyalty. However, I would advise that the follow-up be carried out in an engaging, funny, and educational manner. Become creative in how you can stay in contact with your clients.

There is no better way to put that than the way Dan Kennedy told me, "Be a welcome guest, not an annoying pest."

How can YOU constantly stay in contact with your customer?

6. The Hidden Profit Booster Most Owners Fail to Utilize

One thing I learned the hard way was that making the first sale is the hardest. The other thing that I learned from this experience is that to have a successful business, you need to focus on the existing clients. Build a relationship of trust with your customers, add massive value and make them loyal. These will be the customers that form the very foundation your business will be built on.

Like most small business owners, I made the mistake of focusing on the front end. I was advertising and marketing my business to attract many new customers out there that did not know my business existed. Instead of building a trustworthy relationship with my existing customers and letting them bring in the rest, I pushed them away because I did not give them the attention they deserved. And that, as I said, cost me a lot.

Acquiring a customer is the most expensive part in a business. It's a shame to ignore your current customers after their initial purchase. Make your existing customers like, love, and trust you, so that they become your best advocates.

Don't fall in love with your product or service, fall in love with your customers instead.

The best thing about these six strategies is that it does not matter which tools you use to fulfill these strategies, they will work and grow your business as long as you use them. It does not matter if you follow up by direct mail or if you use the newest email marketing tool, it comes down to the strategy ... not the tools. If you are feeling a bit overwhelmed right now, it is ok. I was too. Just pick one strategy at a time and think of how you can implement it in your business and decide which tool is the best fit for you.

But it all comes down to you and the choices you make, and reading this article was the first step. How you implement what read here in your business in the real world is up to you. However, if you do apply it, then I know you will succeed.

Remember, a strong business is built on a strong foundation. It does not matter how fast your business grows, if the foundation was not well constructed, then the countdown to its collapse has already begun.

The six steps to achieve this are all above.

Master the basics and build a strong foundation.

About Patrick

Patrick Rahn is a Marketing and Business Strategist, best-selling author, CEO of Rahn Consulting and a Certified NLP Practitioner who opooialized in the art and science of the high-achieving business owner.

Before he founded Rahn Consulting, he had worked in over ten different industries and ended up as a structural engineer with a Master's degree. Because of his journey, and by seeing so many different businesses and industries, he was able to find a common denominator of success – one that became his philosophy: *A strong foundation is everything in business as well as your personal life.* This is a philosophy that has enabled him to help his clients find underutilized assets and overlooked opportunities to multiply their profits and expand their freedom. Patrick's goal is to help business owners grow their businesses, thereby increasing their freedom and happiness.

Patrick, in his passionate endeavor to help small-to-midsize businesses reach their full potential, invented a process he calls the "Neuro-Business Strategy Process." In this process, he first incorporates his Infinite Personal Growth Triangle. He analyzes the mindset, paradigms, beliefs systems and goals of the business owner. He then takes his toolbox of proven business tactics and strategies and builds a strategy that fits the business owner, one where they feel happy and free – a company that grows with the business owner on their terms.

Patrick is a best-selling author of the book, *Mindset of Success – How Highly Successful People Think About Goal Setting.* He has also written books alongside other significant personalities such as New York Times Best-Selling Author, Brian Tracy and five-time Emmy Award winner, Nick Nanton. Apart from writing, Patrick is also the CEO of Rahn Consulting, from where his clients receive the best of his business coaching consulting services. For example, he advises clients from all industries, including Banks, Financial Sales & Services and Award-Winning Tech Companies in Germany.

You can connect with Patrick at:
- www.PatrickRahn.com
- Info@patrickrahn.com

CHAPTER 25

HOW DFNDRS LEPT INTO BEING IN THREE COMPLETELY DIFFERENT GIANT STRIDES

WHY IT ALL HAPPENED AND WHERE IT IS GOING

BY PHILIPPA STEEL

DFNDRS is a multi-platform project ranging from experimental youth workshops to internet series to live action TV, animated features, video games, virtual reality and theatre. These are in various stages of development, and all of them relate to protection of the environment.

Key to these is the art and culture of the First Nations, starting with the tribes of the Pacific Northwest in British Columbia, Canada. The root of many things is often in childhood, and the beginning of this particular story dates back many years.

As a small child, I spent a good bit of time watching the carvers at work in Thunderbird park in Victoria. In a very short time, I conceived the desire for my own Thunderbird and proceeded to make enquiries as to how to achieve this. I was informed that this was a time-consuming process, not immediate, and that we would first have to agree a financial transaction. ... with money up front! We dickered for a bit. My allowance at that time was 25 cents a week. The figure of $1.50 was suggested and we settled at $1.25.

Splendid. Carving could commence: it would take some time. Several weeks passed: It seemed an eternity to a six-year old! Finally, I was told that next week all should be ready for me.

I arrived virtually with smoke pouring from my shoes ... to find that some final touches were being made to the paintwork. I bounced about in anticipation. I could see the beautiful small totem as it was finished off and the carver turned it to sign it on the back of its wings. First the left, and then the right – "MUNGO ... MARTIN".

Thus began a lifetime of fascination with the art and culture and stories of the First Nations – initially of the Pacific Northwest, but later all over North America, across Canada, around the USA and all over Mexico.

The next main impelling force shaping this project was years hence when I accidentally went to India for a landmark interview with HH the Dalai Lama. The person originally scheduled to go was unable to at the last moment, and I was the only person available.

So, head over heels into the most foreign of countries on less than 48 hours notice – just long enough to get the necessary visa, pack and fly. Arrival in India at Delhi required immediate ditching of all expectations and entrusting myself and our mission to my Tibetan hosts. The inscription "God Help Us" on our taxi proved predictive: Nothing went according to plan, but everything worked out for the best.

From one side of the continent to the other, up to Sikkim for His Holiness' Kalachakra and back to Dharamsala via Calcutta when it emerged that the original interview plan had been submerged in changes of schedule. From tuk-tuk to trains, planes to motor transport, eventually I found myself in His Holiness' presence.

My instructions were to ask him for guidance as to what one person could do to make a difference to the world. His response was that one should start where one could have the most immediate effect – with oneself. Next, he suggested that I should look around me and see who or what nearby needed help – and start doing whatever I could.

He then said that one had a duty to be happy – as if one were not happy oneself, what could one possibly offer others?

To my comment that there was so much that needed to be done in the world and how could one hope to do much in so little time? He responded: "If not in this lifetime, then the next!"

The third major influence has been my long involvement in developing the work of Jilly Cooper for the screen. In reading her unique books, one is immersed in the world of her characters and their hopes, dreams and adventures. As both crime writer Ian Rankin and Cambridge University literary academic Dr. Ian Patterson also appreciate, since Dickens, no other novelist has come close to compare!

Underpinning everything is the theme that love resolves everything for the best.

In going forward and making choices from loving motivation, eventually the best possible results emerge for all concerned. The good guys triumph and the 'baddies' receive their just deserts. In it all, you see some of the less attractive sides of the heroes, and unsuspected hidden virtues in the villains – and eventually arrive at entirely happy-ever-after solutions by the end of each book. ... and can't wait for the next!!

When ITV unexpectedly backed out at the last moment on this project, we were thrown into some disarray with massive personal losses for me, including my home. And then when this was rapidly succeeded by Sir David Frost's tragic sudden death, I too, came to a temporary dead end.

What was to be done?

So I looked about me, and the **DFNDRS** project jumped into being.

Largely due to the efforts of May Street Productions and the Educating Through Change Society, our first experimental youth workshop takes place on Denman Island, BC this summer – it is an exciting time!!! Other elements are steaming ahead, but this is our starting point to save the planet. A first small step to help create a world of peace and joy.

Everything is inter-related – rooted, implanted, immersed and growing on the land and in the oceans, in the lakes, the rivers and streams. To survive and thrive, we must care for the earth and all who live in it, and there lies our happiness. Our starting point is to care fundamentally for ourselves – to eat and drink well, exercise with delight and ensure our individual good health.

DFNDRS is taking off in the Pacific Northwest, cradle of other well-known sustainable ventures too. But the launch of this one and its ancillaries beyond is from the traditions of the marvellous First Nations cultures and their magnificent, exciting traditions in story, music, dance and art. There is much to reveal … and a lot of fun to come.

Watch this space, but meantime the basic recipe for health and happiness is a version of do as you would be done by – and quite likely you may find heaven on earth by making earth a heaven.

Look after the earth, and it will look after you.
Saving the world is crucial for us all, and if not now, then when?

I can only wish you the peaceable best in every way.

About Philippa

Philippa Steel has extensive experience in development, raising and syndicating finance, production and delivery of projects on all media platforms, including film, television, theatre, journalism, print, publishing, photography, concerts, internet and exhibitions.

Her qualifications are:
+ BA – University of British Columbia
+ Dip. Tech. – British Columbia Institute of Technology
+ Life Member – NUJ

Philippa has worked in both public and private sectors, from North America to Europe and Asia, writing and producing. Notable examples include production for the Canadian Habitat Secretariat for the United Nations, the English Tourist Board and the London Docklands Development Corporation – as well as her landmark interview with HH the Dalai Lama in Dharamsala.

Numerous theatrical ventures with Pola Jones such as *The Nerd, Neville's Island, The Life and Death of Arturo Ui, Forbidden Planet, Little Shop of Horrors* and more. In addition, she has orchestrated many varied television development projects, most extensively the work of Jilly Cooper with the late Sir David Frost, OBE.

Philippa is a supporter of the Danson Chair in Anthropology at the Museum of Northern Arizona, and the Kensington and Chelsea Music Society among others.

She also supports youth in changing attitudes, inspiring new ways to take a stand via their creations in compelling cutting-edge media – art, music, drama, dance, documentary, video, games and internet, etc. through the DFNDRS of the Environment project. (https://www.facebook.com/EvironmentDFNDRS/)

Contact information for Philippa is:
• Email: philippasteel@hotmail.com

Philippa supports fundamental good health through free information and HEADSTART app at:
• www.changeofmind.ca

For further information on DFNDRS youth workshops, please go to:
• www.dfndrsoftheenvironment.ca

CHAPTER 26

THE ART OF MOVING FORWARD
GET UNSTUCK IN SEVEN STEPS

BY JACKIE SMITH

I was so curious! So, I did some research on the word "art". I learned that Art means skill, the ability to do something. So, I call this chapter, "The Art of Moving Forward" because it requires much talent and skill to take the steps to move forward and become the artists we are meant to be. Let me explain my point of view, I believe we are all made by a Creator. Whoever that creator may be for you, God, the Universe, Science, etc. This is a matter of your own beliefs; nevertheless, we can all agree an artist made each and every one of us. Therefore, I invite you to wander in my theory that says we own the gift of being creative. I was even more curious and did some research on the word, 'creative'. I learned that 'creative' means: possessing the power to make something.

We all have this special power to do something with our lives. We are meant to add something wonderful to the world. Whatever we want to create we can create, it is up to us. I hope we agree, so far.

Often, we don't use this power enough. In fact, we often forget we have this special talent at all. It is there – all we need to do is tap in to it. This leaves us to live a life with no purpose. And, that is not an option!

I am here to remind you of your powers and to help you tap in to them.

Let's begin with a requisite to be eligible to be a participant. Think of it like a club rule. The key word is *Desire*. It is the requirement for accepting the challenge of moving forward. You must want to move forward! ... truly and deeply feeling the need for change. With this revelation alone, you have accomplished at least half, according to my calculations.

I will tell you a bit about me, so you understand where I am coming from. I was an only child, living in the 1970s, with no electronics. I spent loads of time alone and in silence. I had full on conversation with my imaginary friends. The dolls were my friends, we would often have tea.

My home. It was so quiet that I had the time to hear the voices in my head ... in a good way! Today, I recognize it as the voice of intuition. It sounded like a faint murmur in my ear. Hints, I imagined, of some higher power that helped guide me through my life. Kindly assisting me to move past things that no longer served me.

Gently nudging me towards what is best for me. I found a sisterhood in this voice and kept the practice of this power. It has helped me throughout my life. And I would like to share it with you.

I believe that life speaks to us in whispers. These are the messages that the Universe sends. They are announcements that say something has to change. I think we can all hear them; we just need to learn to listen. I think we all come into the world with a purpose, a special art. It is a gift provided by the Universe, and what you do with it is your own gift to humanity.

Have you ever felt stuck and did not know what to do? I think we all have come to this realization before we make a decision to change our lives.

Are you ready to move forward? Do you want to live the life you desire? If 'yes' is your answer, then this practical guide is for you. I know that coincidences do not exist. Rather, they are opportunities that grow, based on the accumulation of your efforts. The decisions and steps you take today are what the future will be built on. There is a reason you are still reading my chapter and you are about to find out.

Through my years of experience and studies, I have come up with seven steps to unstick you. A practical Life-Coaching lesson you can give to yourself.

1. LISTEN

We all have a story to tell. You want to be heard and acknowledged. Some stories are nice. But then, some stories are often paralyzing and bad. They are like loaded bags of dramas from past generations that do not belong to you. Perhaps a teacher, friend or relative told you "no" and you believed them. This formed a limiting belief. I got curious again, and researched 'limiting belief'. I learned it means to hold something as true in your heart that constrains you.

You must have the desire to take the steps in moving forward ... each time further and further away from these limiting beliefs. You must be willing and open to changing your thoughts and leave your comfort zone. When you change how you see things, the things you see change. Listen to your inner dialogue, "WHAT IS ON YOUR MIND?"

Take some time to find silence. Notice how you talk to yourself. Your words have power. Shhhhh, do not judge, just listen!

These are five ways you can find silence:

(a). Meditate for one minute at any time. Everyone has one minute! Close your eyes and breathe deeply. Inhale and exhale three times. Listen to your heartbeat. Smile with every breath.

(b). Practice yoga. This ancient Asian practice is proven to be good for your health.

(c). Take a warm bath. There is a natural healing property that is in water. It comes from our Mother Earth.

(d). Be in touch with nature. I like to practice "grounding". My research says that Grounding is the practice of walking barefoot on the grass. The healing properties of the Earth take pains away. This philosophy says that the Universe balances your energy, leaving the good within you and discarding what you do not need. Or hug a tree.

(e). Pray. Faith is key.

2. ASK

Are you ready to ask yourself Powerful questions? I did some more research and learned that Powerful questions are those questions that make you explore the depths of your being.

It is your job to answer the question truthfully.

At this point, ask yourself, "WHO AM I?"

Shhhhh ... do not judge, just listen!

It is the time when you have to think deeply about your answers. They are to be found in your silence, the most private place within you.

I know it is easier said than done! The mind does play tricks on you. Outsmart your mind by simply observing what feeling come up for you. This gives you clues about what your answers are.

3. ORGANIZE

Based on your phenomenal ability to listen to yourself and truthfully answer the powerful questions, now you should feel more mindful. I did even more research, and learned that Mindful means to notice. Your job is to be aware! The powerful question is: "WHAT DO I WANT?"

Take your time. It is your job to make a list and prioritize. It is important to be precise as this step shapes the steps to come. It is starting to mold your action plan. My research says that an action plan is a proposed strategy or course of action.

Ideas to organize priorities:

(a). Take a pencil, a sheet of paper and make a list. Something magical happens when you write something down.

(b). Surround yourself with people you admire. Be mindful of the company you keep.

(c). Forgive others, not because they deserve it, but because you deserve peace. You will feel much lighter and easier to move forward.

(d). Consistency is key. When you think, say and do is the same, the Universe conspires to make your wish come true.

4. FOCUS

You are taking the correct steps towards the path of your choosing. You are carefully selecting what you pick to focus on. Remember that you are the master of your life. You dictate what you want or do not want in your life. Look at your list and powerfully ask yourself, "WHERE DO I BEGIN?" Shhhhh, do not judge, just listen!

Once you have decided what to focus on, it becomes time to take action.

Celebrate both your victories and the challenges. Celebrating victories is easy and obvious. But challenges are always peeking through and it is a sure sign that you are trying. This is where a good attitude is most important in order to thrive.

I firmly believe that human beings can achieve what they want. You must be prepared to take the steps you need to achieve it. No one will do the job for you. It is that simple.

Five things you can do to help focus on your goal:

(a). Strive to be in the company of people with similar goals.

(b). Study the topic that interests you. Soak up wisdom.

(c). Use your words carefully. Words have power! Choose

positive words to help you grow.

(d). Continue to meditate. Silence organizes your thoughts.

(e). Do not complain about what you do not have, rather, be grateful for what you do have.

5. PERSIST

Do not give up! You have come this far. You have gained clarity to determine which direction you want to pursue. You have set goals and are determined to achieve them. At this moment, take a look at your habits. You have become more aware of the patterns of behavior that benefit you. This is part of the awareness process: Instead of being a victim, you turn into the hero of your own story.

Habits fill up your day and days fill up your life. Small changes transform your life. The powerful question is: "WHAT DO I NEED TO DO, to make my goals happen?"

Five activities you can practice to be consistent:

(a). Celebrate small goals. This is a process that is achieved in parts. Do not wait to celebrate in the future. Celebrate today, now!

(b). Place reminders and motivational notes in places where you know you'll see them – on your desk, in your car, or on your mirror.

(c). Take note of your internal dialogue. Make sure you keep a positive mind. Thank you, thank you, thank you is what I say when a negative thought is interrupted. I feel evil is wiped out when I choose to be thankful.

(d). Write about your process in a journal.

(e). Keep a positive attitude.

6. BE GRATEFUL

Pause and be thankful. Have an attitude of gratitude. Recognize the steps you have taken and how much you have progressed when you appreciate what you already have. Instead of complaining about what you do not have, you will always have more than enough. Start with what you have and move forward.

The powerful question is: "WHAT ARE YOU GRATEFUL FOR?"

Five Ways to be thankful:

(a). Put your hand on your chest. Do you feel your heartbeat? Be thankful you are alive and for the sound of your breathing.

(b). Be thankful for your home, family, good friends, health, water, food and love.

(c). Say "thank you" for no apparent reason.

(d). Help others; perform acts of empathy.

(e). Be thankful for the planet we live in.

7. TRANSFORM YOURSELF

This step is special; it is what you want to achieve and sustain. You realize your truth and have risen to a new level. You now know what you do and do not want. You also know what you need to do in order to achieve your goals. It's a great revelation. I am convinced that the steps we make today build our future. If you improve by 1% every day, in a year's time you will be in a position that is 365% better.

The beautiful thing about transformation is that it can be repeated. Moving forward is your every day job. You can transform as many times as you want in your life. The powerful question is: "WHAT IS NEXT?" Shhhhh, don't judge, just listen!

Move forward! Reinvent yourself! The world awaits you. Are you curious? I am.

About Jackie

Jackie Smith was born October 1, 1967 in Tegucigalpa, Honduras. As a child, she would spend her time writing and illustrating books. She lived with her Honduran Mother and French Father.

She lived in Honduras until she graduated the American School in 1985.

Coming from a family of Bankers, she naturally went to Bentley University in Waltham, Massachusetts. She graduated in 1989 with a Bachelor's Degree in Marketing. Following her passion for studies, she continued on to Fairleigh Dickinson University in Madison, New Jersey where she earned her Master's degree in Positive Psychology. She graduated *Summa Cum Laude* and was a Teacher's Assistant during her second year of Graduate studies.

Fascinated by the world of happiness, she deepened her knowledge by studying mostly spiritual leaders, including Jesus, Deepak Chopra, Don Miguel Ruiz, Gandhi and Buddha to name a few. She travelled extensively around the world to extend her knowledge of other cultures. Her father's French influence brings her to France often to visit friends and family.

Immersed in the world of well-being, she decided to return to her roots and love of writing. She joined forces with *ESTILO Magazine* from Honduras in 2010. She writes a monthly magazine column and a blog on their online magazine. (http://blogs.revistaestilo.net/life-coaching/)

In 2004, Jackie decided to enroll In University of Miami Coaching Program. She is a Certified Life Coach, by the International Coaching Federation.

In 2006, Jackie wrote *The Art of Moving Forward* and began a career in motivational speaking. She has shared the stage, radio show and has a Monthly column with former CNN news anchor, and now motivational leader, Ismael Cala.

In 2007, Jackie came full circle and became the dream she wished for as a child. She became a Best-Selling author by co-authoring with Brian Tracy in the popular book *Ready, Set, Go.*

Jackie plans on continuing her route to success by empowering others with her expert knowledge.

She lives in Miami, Florida and enjoys peaceful, quiet time at home.

- lifecoachjackiesmith@gmail.com
- Facebook: JACKIE SMITH
- Instagram: jackiesmith67
- Twitter: Jackie smith@smithjackie67

CHAPTER 27

ENOUGH ABOUT ME, LET'S TALK ABOUT YOU

BY GARY KIEPER

You can have everything in life you want, if you'll just help other people get what they want.
~ Zig Ziglar

When you hear words like selfless, servant, and unselfish, what images come to mind? I think of Jesus, moms, dads, teachers, or maybe my high school wrestling coach. But what words would you use to describe someone in a sales position, such as a banker, financial advisor, or insurance agent? **My guess is it's not one of the above. Why is that?**

In today's world, social media has made everything "about me", inundating us with countless posts about new cars, fancy vacations, or anything that makes our lives seem more interesting. Everywhere, we are being sold the erroneous notion that it's "all about me." It's to the point where we feel most people are not genuine in their posts. In fact, we know life isn't as glorious as most people make it seem.

Communication has changed. In just the past 20 years, we've gone from live telephone and face-to-face conversations to texting, emails, and voicemails. We've lost the ability to engage in meaningful dialogue. We no longer make an effort to master the skills of reading body language and facial expressions, intuiting the emotions or motives of others, or interpreting other non-verbal signals. This change hasn't just affected our personal lives, but our business lives as well. We spend more time texting and emailing than we do talking.

If you're in sales, and let's face it, we're all selling something, it's time to say enough about me, let's talk about you!

THE PROBLEM WITH "ALL ABOUT ME"

I have surveyed, interviewed, and communicated with thousands of sales professionals, and the one common thread amongst nearly all is that they seem to have trouble staying focused on the customer. They start out with every intention of being customer-centered, but shortly after the conversation starts, they drift back to products and services or features and benefits (more 'me' statements). They fail to truly listen to what the prospect needs and rush to solve problems before they have enough information.

Why does this transition back to "me" occur? Simply put, we've lost touch with how to effectively communicate with people. Hard as we try, we slip back into trying to accomplish our own agenda instead of listening to and learning about other people and their problems.

This creates the following issues:

- The quick transition back to "me" eliminates the ability to gather more information about the customer.
- By trying to solve problems too soon, we appear as a "know-it-all".
- We've failed to show how much we care by focusing on how much we know.
- We make the conversation all about us and our own personal agenda.

TELL ME MORE ABOUT YOU

Let's use dating as an example. When you went on the first date with your significant other, you spent hours talking to each other, and the time seemed to fly by as you listened intently to every word that was spoken. You asked questions about his or her family, education, work goals, religious beliefs, favorite songs, or greatest memories.

Imagine how different things might have been if instead you'd had a one-sided conversation that focused squarely on "all about me." Or, what if you shared something painful and before explaining the entire story, your date cut you off and told you what a mistake you made and how the entire event could have been prevented in the first place.

Or better yet, what if he or she asked you to marry them on the first date!

Chances are you would never have led the conversation with any of those things during the relationship-building stage. However, this is exactly what happens in sales when we don't ask the right questions, or when we fail to learn enough about our prospect before presenting a solution and asking for a commitment.

HOW DOES DATING RELATE TO SELLING?

Now let's imagine that during an initial meeting with a prospect, they share painful details of the existing relationship with your competitor. They share with you how they aren't being serviced as promised and the product doesn't perform as advertised. At this point, you have two choices: You can either tell them how great your service is and how your product will deliver (solve their problem now) OR you can decide to ask more questions about how their service needs aren't being met and specifically, how the product fails in performance.

Just as with dating, the same principles apply when talking to a customer. The more questions you ask the customer, the more you make it about them, and the more you listen to what they say, the higher the likelihood that they'll share sensitive and critical information. Much like dating, you need to earn trust. Then it's how you use the information that can make or break the relationship.

THE POWER OF A SELFLESS PROCESS

selfless ~ *having or showing great concern for other people and little or no concern for yourself*

One of my greatest joys is teaching people how to create a selfless process as it relates to sales. It doesn't matter what you are selling; letting the prospect know exactly how the process works is invaluable and puts the focus on them. Let me give you a quick example. Suppose

I was selling insurance to a business owner and I was granted an initial meeting. Most sales people will start the meeting by talking about their company and why they feel they can help. They will ask some general questions and build dialogue based on responses. However, the amount of information they can extract from the customer is only as good as the amount of trust they've built. The greater the trust, the greater the response. Talking about ourselves and our company doesn't necessarily build earned. What happens if the customer doesn't want to divulge critical information because they don't know why you need it or how you are going to use it? In other words, what if they don't feel confident giving you the information? What if their pride doesn't allow them to admit they have problems?

This is where having a rock-solid selfless process pays huge dividends for both parties. Instead of starting a meeting out with "all about me" statements, start with telling the customer about your process, why you do certain things, and how they can benefit. Make the conversation about them and how you help solve problems.

So then, let's assume the small talk is over and you're ready to move into fact finding. Instead of starting with "me" statements, try starting with something like, *"Mr. Prospect, I'm not sure if you are like most of my customers, but they tell me one of the things they enjoy most about working with me is the process I go through. Is it ok if I share with you how my process works so you'll have a better understanding of what to expect during our time together today?"* At this point I always pause and wait for permission to continue. (GREAT!)

Once the customer agrees, proceed.

"First, I'm going to ask you questions about your business so I have a crystal-clear understanding of your needs. Some questions I'll ask might be personal in nature but I want you to know upfront that I'll only ask for information to help me determine whether I can be of service to you. If at any time, you'd like to know why I need certain information or how I'm going to use it, please let me know and I'll gladly explain.

Second, if I feel I might be able to help, I'll explain more about myself and my company and how I've assisted other customers'.

Third, if you like what you hear, I'll ask to review your existing insurance program to compare coverages based on the information you provided. I'll be looking for gaps in coverage or possibly over-insured areas within your limits.

Fourth, I'll prepare a detailed proposal outlining the areas I feel I can help, and I'll set a time to review the proposal directly with you.

Finally, if you feel I've brought value to your business, I'll ask you to allow me to become your advisor. Does that sound fair?"

In a nutshell:

- Start with a trust building statement that's focused on them.
- Ask for permission to continue.
- Tell them you have a process.
- Explain the process thoroughly, point by point, including why you might need sensitive information. This is a huge trust building statement.
- End by letting them know you will ask for their business.

HOW DOES A SELFLESS PROCESS BUILD TRUST?

Consider starting a selfless conversation using a process like I've described above. I've found that once I explain the process, customer responses to probing questions are much deeper and more valuable. Why? Because trust is being built on a rock-solid foundation. We've demonstrated consistency. We've already explained our process. When we follow it, the customer already knows what to expect so there are no surprises. Trust is gained by doing what we said we were going to do. Simple but effective!

How else do we build trust? Look at our process and pay attention to two statements:

- *"I'm not sure if you are like most of my customers, but they tell me one of the things they enjoy about working with me is the process I go through."*
- *"If I feel I might be able to help, I'll explain more about me and my company and how I've helped similar customers."*

Let's break the first sentence down and explain why this simple statement helps to build trust. The phrase, "I'm not sure if you are like most of my customers" does two things. First, it says you're not making any assumptions about their unique situation. This is HUGE! Everyone wants to feel special and unique. This small statement helps accomplish exactly that. Second, it lets them know you have other customers. Another small win.

The second statement is strong as well. The phrase, *"If I feel I might be able to help"* reinforces no assumptions are being made and their time won't be wasted by talking about "me" if it isn't necessary.

Some other helpful trust-building statements:

- I'm not sure if I can help (I'm not making any assumptions).
- I don't know enough about your unique situation to know whether I can help, but I would welcome an opportunity to learn more (I need more information about you).
- My customers tell me the three biggest problems we solve are… (This statement has two benefits: The first is, it's basically a customer testimonial. People believe what other people say, not necessarily what you say. The second is, if these issues exist for your prospect, this shows you to be the expert in your field.)
- Can I give you an example of how I've helped other companies solve similar issues? (This reinforces you're an expert. You've seen similar problems before and have had positive outcomes.)

Remember, the greater the trust, the more valuable the responses are from your customer. As you continue to build and show value, your customer will give you more ways in which you can help them.

SUMMARY

Living in an "all about me" era makes it difficult to effectively communicate. We've learned to put ourselves and our desires in front of the needs of others. This exists in both our personal and professional lives. We've become desensitized to talking about ourselves.

My goal with this chapter is to help you consider how you use language and whether it's self-serving or selfless. Many people believe they are trying to help others, only to learn they are only trying to meet their own agenda. We must re-invent ourselves in how we communicate with others. If nothing else, write down what you say to customers and ask yourself, *"Is this about them or is it about me?"* Remember, it's not what you say that counts, but rather what they hear!

Try dating your prospects. Get to know them on a deeper level. Court them, serve them, even if they aren't your customer…yet. Building trust doesn't happen by accident. Be intentional and make it all about them.

About Gary

Gary Kieper Jr. helps his clients achieve their sales and business goals by providing sales training, coaching, and customized customer-facing sales language. He created the Selfless Sales™ Process to help clients build deeper and more meaningful relationships through advanced communication skills with customers.

Gary is the founder of Kieper Sales Solutions and has spent the past 20+ years learning, teaching, and transforming the sales process.

In 2014, Gary's blog was selected by Docurated, a company that offers the fastest and simplest way for sales and marketing teams to find and use content, as one of their top 50 "must read" blogs on consultative selling saying, "Gary Kieper believes all of the traditional sales strategies are necessary for business success. But, he also believes that driving sales rests on adding value to the relationship by educating and helping prospects understand their problems and showing them how you've helped solve those same problems for other clients. He has consultative sales at the core of his business philosophy and it shines through his blog posts as well."

In 2015, Gary became certified as an Exit Planning Advisor helping business owners eliminate risk while maximizing value as they prepare to transition out of their business. That same year, he was certified as a Family Business Advisor where he helps family-owned businesses transition from one generation to the next. Both certifications allow Gary to fully engage with clients on an array of issues that are not just sales related.

Gary, a national speaker, is a member of The National Association of Experts, Writers & Speakers and routinely speaks at national sales meetings.

You can connect with Gary at:
- Gary@SelflessSales.com
- www.SelflessSales.com
- www.twitter.com/GaryKieper
- www.linkedin.com/in/garykieper/

CHAPTER 28

TEN STEPS TO REGAIN YOUR PERSONAL POWER

BY JANET MCKEE

What do you want for your life? Why haven't you yet achieved your dreams? What has stopped you from reaching the level of success in life that you desire? There is no need to feel frustrated any longer. You do have the power over your own fate.

What I'm about to teach you, is exactly what you need to triumph over any obstacles and finally achieve your goals and aspirations and begin to improve your life, starting NOW!

I'm not immune to experiencing challenges and struggles. After achieving solid success early in my career at a Fortune 500 company where I was promoted faster than my peers, I made a bold move into sales. Thinking I was invincible after graduating at the top of my class in school and enjoying corporate success, I hadn't yet experienced failure. Soon, I found myself struggling to make my numbers and floundering to close deals. After incorporating stress-management techniques that I now teach, I focused on my goal. Within a short time, I achieved top sales in a multi-billion-dollar organization where I single-handedly sold over $20million in products and services in one year alone.

Several years later, again thinking I was invincible, I made a new leap into entrepreneurship. Soon, I found myself struggling. Why? How could I be so successful in the past but again be worrying about generating enough revenue to grow my business and pay the bills?

With the concerns of leaving the corporate world along with challenges developing in my marriage, I ended up with an autoimmune disorder. Hitting rock bottom in all areas of my life - along with my doctors telling me that there was no hope to resolve my illness, I began to search for answers. After a few years, I resolved my health challenge and have been medication free for over 20 years, which the doctors had said was impossible. Becoming passionate about helping others, I attended a wellness school affiliated with Columbia University and have since helped countless clients resolve debilitating and even life-threatening illnesses. What I've witnessed, however, was that some people followed through with my advice and achieved their goals while others did not follow through.   So, I wanted to understand why.

TURN OBSTACLES INTO OPPORTUNITIES

In researching the psychology behind goal achievement, I discovered powerful secrets to living a good life. The most exciting fact I learned is that people have greater control over their destiny than they might believe. I am passionate about helping others and have dedicated my life to guiding people to enjoy successful lives.

Through the years, each struggle I encountered taught me invaluable lessons that made me the successful professional I am today.   Now the owner of three thriving businesses, a public speaker, an author, a High Performance™ consultant with perfect health and enjoying true happiness in my life, I realize I wouldn't be where I am today without overcoming past challenges. How did I do it? What is the secret to a life of success and fulfillment? It comes down to one thing – managing our inner environment.

This transformation can begin with some simple questions: In what areas of your life have you overcome challenges in the past? What amazing lessons did you learn that have made you stronger and wiser and helped you accomplish more? Contemplate that and discover how the focus of your thinking helped you reach the next level of your life.

CHANGE YOUR MINDSET, CHANGE YOUR LIFE

People are living a nightmare when they believe their lives are a result of causes other than their own thoughts and actions. Much of what happens to you is largely a result of your thoughts, beliefs and feelings. *To improve your life and become a new person, the basis of all your thoughts must change.* Your thoughts begin to change when you start to cultivate *new ideas.* Like spring crocus in colorful bloom, new empowering ideas inevitably will blossom if you follow these ten important steps.

1) Desire and intend to change and succeed.

Are you willing to do what it takes to realize your dreams? What do you think and believe about yourself? Do you realize that this creates your reality? Do you know that you deserve to think amazing things about yourself? So many people don't believe that they can or deserve to have a fantastic life. They see themselves as always struggling financially or always being overweight and unhealthy. Or, they feel their life is "fine" and refuse to make it extraordinary.

I've taught thousands how to overcome limiting beliefs, how to change old harmful thought patterns, how to gain clarity, energy, confidence, motivation and influence; and how to take the critical steps to turn fear into something that provides benefits over inhibitions. To gain this life-changing insight, many consult with me privately, hire me to speak to their organizations, or gain online access to my multitude of courses and information that is available at www.sanaview.com. *One of the most powerful concepts that will impact your ability to realize your dreams, however, is what I am about to teach you here.*

In my other teachings, you learn *how to raise your energy level to improve your inner environment,* so that it matches what you desire in your outer life. At my 52-acre historic landmark organic farm, SanaView Farms, my farm manager knows the importance of energy and how it impacts our plants. If I'm in a grumpy mood, he chases me out of the greenhouse – especially when seedlings are being started. He says positive moods are required when planting seeds or else it stunts their growth. What we are doing here in this chapter is *planting the seeds of positive creation* and watch them blossom into the amazing being that you are. As Robert Louis Stevenson said, *"Don't judge each day by the harvest you reap but by the seeds that you plant."*

Please don't wait until some future goal is achieved to be happy. How often have you heard people say, "Oh, I'll be happy when I get the new job, the new relationship, the money, the car or the house?" They strive and struggle with negative energy thinking that the more they stress out the sooner they will get there and get happy. *Get happy and uplift your inner environment first and your dreams will more easily flow to you. How do you do that?*

The key here is to understand the power of your imagination and of intense visualization to create not only a mental image of what you want, but also to get the feeling as if it is already your reality. From this, you will move mountains, because the energy that you feel on the inside is reflected in your life on the outside. Napolean Hill once said, *"Imagination is the most marvelous, miraculous, inconceivably powerful force the world has ever known."*

2) Create a mental image of what you want.

If you are ill, you see yourself as ill. If you say, "I am healthy and strong", the neural pathways in your brain begin to replicate this, you begin to identify with it, and soon your life reflects this. As Neville Goddard wrote, *"If you will not imagine yourself as other than what you are, then you remain as you are."* If you think you are broke or struggling in your professional career, what will your life continue to reflect back to you? This impacts your social and intimate life, financial state, and spiritual life. If you say, "I am smart, I am loveable, I am financially secure," and *get the feeling* as if you are, your entire life will show you that it's true.

The pathways of your brain are actually arranged by what you associate with; rich or poor, healthy or sick, a success or failure. You see this as the truth. Your concept of yourself can be observed by your reactions to life, which illustrate where you live in your mind. If you "know" you are broke, how will you react when an unexpected bill arrives? If instead you *felt* secure, you would look at it calmly and find a solution.

3) Get the **feeling** through visualization as if what you want is real.

When you desire to be better than you are, you can create in your mind the ideal, and then live with the thoughts and feelings as if it is already your reality. When this becomes your dominant feeling, positive results are inevitable.

Ask yourself why you want each goal. Continue to ask until you arrive at the feeling reason. For example, if you want to earn more money, ask why. Possibly the reason is that you want to buy a bigger house. Why do you want the bigger house? Maybe you want comfort and security. It is actually the *feeling* of comfort and security that you are after.

You must know what it feels like to be healthy to experience good health. You must know what it feels like to be secure to experience financial security. To become a new and greater version of you, imagine and feel as if you are already what you want to be.

4) Have trust and faith.

You must know in your heart that positive feelings that come from a vivid imagination will create positive outcomes. It is faith that can truly move mountains. John Muir said, *"The power of imagination makes us infinite."*

5) Release the current reality.

Will you be the ruler of your imagination or a slave to current reality? In standard living, we have no control over our imagination and instead react to what we experience around us. It may seem hard to ignore reality, but when you practice and develop this skill, it becomes a habit and therefore easier.

Direct your attention from what you don't want to what you do want. If you worry about money, don't focus on lack but instead the excitement of finding new ways to make more. If you are ill, imagine instead of enjoying vibrant health. Crowd out the unpleasant reality with the exhilarating feeling of achieving your goals. Fill your mind with visualizations and your heart with joyous feelings.

6) Use concentration and discipline to focus your attention with intention.

The results will correlate to the degree to which you focus. The results depend on your *inner force* or your ability to concentrate. "May the force be with you!" You must persist in generating this feeling and soon the mental image will become your reality. Your ideal life will only be realized once you imagine yourself as living that life. This is deliberate intent.

You are already creating but without intent. In the past, whatever you saw, you thought had just happened by circumstance and that you had little to no control. Now you must live with the wisdom of creating a new life by envisioning a better reality and getting the feeling as if it is already true.

7) Choose a feeling that is natural.

If you create a mental image of your new life and capture the feeling as if it is already your reality, *it should feel natural to you*. I could try to envision myself as an NFL quarterback, but that somehow doesn't feel natural. Neville Goddard wrote, *"When you can call up at will whatsoever image you please, when the forms of your imagination are as vivid to you as the forms of nature, you are master of your fate."*

I teach often about the importance of raising your inner energy. Notice that this is what's happening. When you imagine your ideal life as real and it feels natural to you, your energy is uplifted. When you understand the power of your imagination, you hold the key to living your best life.

Is this easy? Yes.
Can anyone do this? Yes.
Will everyone do this? No.

To the general public, this seems like fruitless fantasy. Have you noticed how the general public lives? Most people spend an average of four hours per day in front of the TV (which equates to 13 years of their lives) eating processed chemical-laden foods, living in fear and lack. Do you want to be like the unfulfilled general population? Or, do you want to open your mind to new ideas of progress?

If Columbus accepted the world as flat, where would we be today? If the leaders of the technology companies did not envision a world where we could walk around with computers in the palm of our hand, where would we be today? Albert Einstein stated, *"Imagination is more important than knowledge."*

8) Develop a deep burning desire to reach your goal.

Where have you done this in the past? When I was a young professional, I remember seeing a woman who looked like me driving a Mercedes. I thought to myself, "That should be me." Soon, I had a deep desire to earn more so I passionately pursued a high-powered sales position. This was the job in which I earned more money than I thought was possible at that point in my career. One paycheck alone was $150,000. The year I was pregnant with my son, I made over $400,000, and this was 20 years ago!

9) Have fun with this process.

When my son was very small he drew a Hawaiian picture. I'll never forget it because we had it on the wall of our home office that we shared. The picture was just a string of colored lights that represented to him a Hawaiian luau. I remember at first thinking, I can't see us going to Hawaii any time soon. Soon enough, we ended up there and had the most fabulous time of our lives that we still laugh about today.

10) Experience the feeling daily.

Where you go in your imagination, you will be in reality soon enough. You have the power to alter the course of your future. The choice is yours: You can be distracted by the objective view of your current reality or you can deliberately create subjective views based on your imagination. Each day withdraw into the subjective that you create in your mind's eye and become absorbed in the feeling as if that subjective view is your reality.

YOUR EMPOWERMENT IS IN YOUR HANDS

Are you ready to take full responsibility for your life? Are you ready to stop blaming others or outside circumstances? I'm not saying that these weren't real and haven't had a huge impact on your life in the past. What I am suggesting is that you now become empowered to take back control of your entire life. Someone else less enlightened may look at how your life improves simply as luck. You are now wiser than this because you don't have to hope for good luck. You have complete control.

I HAVE HANDED YOU BACK YOUR PERSONAL POWER!

May you now not only Embrace a Better Life,
but embrace the life of your dreams.

About Janet

Janet McKee, wellness expert, motivational speaker, author and founder of Sanaview, is on a mission to inspire and teach you proven and effective ways to **Embrace a Better Life**; a life that is richer, happier, healthier, and more fulfilling. "Sana" is Latin for "health and wellness" and her organization provides a "view" into enjoyable ways to dramatically improve your life.

After experiencing tremendous success in the corporate environment and obtaining her MBA from the University of Pittsburgh, Ms. McKee became passionate about helping others. So, she pursued a health and wellness degree with a school affiliated with Columbia University. After working for many years to help people achieve greater levels of well-being, Ms. McKee expanded her expertise by researching how psychology impacts a person's ability to achieve personal and professional goals. Based on this work, she has achieved the status of being one of only 200 elite Certified High Performance Coaches™ in the world and has received the honor of being awarded membership into the National Association of Experts, Writers and Speakers.

Ms. McKee is a vibrant and inspirational speaker who is known for captivating audiences through the use of real-life stories and anecdotal accounts that engage, entertain, uplift and empower people with real solutions that they can begin to use immediately to realize their dreams.

Whether you consult with Ms. McKee directly, or hire her to speak to your organization, or peruse her multitude of online courses and inspirations, you are certain to become more knowledgeable, uplifted and motivated to improve your life.

As the founder and executive producer of SanaView, Ms. McKee has released her own book titled, *Fabulous Recipes for Vibrant Health*, and is the executive producer of the award-winning documentary, Bethany's Story, about the healing power of food. Because of her passion for healthy living, Ms. McKee spends her free time helping to develop SanaView Farms, her 52-acre historic landmark organic farm nestled in the Laurel Mountains of Pennsylvania. There, she teaches ways to regenerate our land and our health through natural living and eating. A true powerhouse of positive energy and motivation, Ms. McKee is poised to dramatically improve the lives of everyone she touches.

Teaching proven methods to achieve greater levels of energy, engagement, joy and confidence are the keys to her success in helping others.

To learn more visit:
- www.sanaview.com
- youtube.com/sanaview
- facebook.com/JanetMcKeefan
- facebook.com/sanaview
- Janet can be reached at: janet@sanaview.com

CHAPTER 29

THE GENESIS OF SUSTAINABLE SUCCESS: ATTRACT IT!

BY DOUG HANSON

In 1993, I was in my early 30's with three small children, and unbeknownst to me, one more on the way. Success and leadership had become very important to me, primarily so I could provide for my family and influence their lives for the better. More than anything, I wanted to have the wisdom and skills to effectively lead my wife and children into a life full of *worldly successes*, executed on the *bedrock of character*, and balanced with *spiritual purpose*. As I was journaling one day, I captured a fairly obvious but profound distinction that really sent me a wake-up call. I wrote, *"You can't give away what you don't have!"* In other words, if I really wanted to help my children live a full life, rich with purpose and meaning, I needed to do it myself first. Yikes! How do I do that?

So, I became a sponge for all the personal development material I could get my hands on. With a specific outcome in mind, like health, wealth, or relationships, or a specific skill like investing, influence, or time management, I would seek out the best person I could learn from and model them. I especially gravitated towards speakers and authors that aligned with my interests in balancing faith and family with success and service. Some of my favorites were Brian Tracy, Jim Rohn, Dr. Nido Qubein, Zig Ziglar, Brian Biro, and Tony Robbins. Later, I set goals to meet some of these great achievers in person, which I did several times over. I even worked with a few, including seven consecutive years with Tony Robbins as a guest facilitator and speaker at his famous *Life Mastery University* in Hawaii.

The thing that impressed me most about these thought leaders was their giving nature. They didn't necessarily make it easy to gain access to them, but once you proved you were worthy, whether it be through creativity or tenacity, they were all more than willing to share their knowledge and wisdom.

I remember the first time I met Dr. Qubein. I remember it so well because something he shared with me that day was the genesis of a completely different approach to life and success for me.

After that meeting, I completely shifted my focus. I spent less time looking for more strategies to model and more time developing and galvanizing my own philosophies. There is a big difference between the two. I realized that every new strategy I adopted carried the overhead of more and more transactional to-dos, whereas every new philosophy I embraced brought more peace of mind and a better quality of life, (and here's the best part), without any sacrifice to my results. In fact, my results improved as well.

The question I asked Dr. Qubein was, ***"If you could only give one nugget of advice to a person who's willing to do whatever you say for a successful and fulfilling life, what would it be?"***

Without a moment's hesitation he said, *"Doug, show me your **To-Do** list."*

I couldn't wait to show him my To-Do list. I had recently read several books on time management and attended an intensive goal setting workshop, so my To-Do list was exceptionally well thought through. I often joked that it was *organized, alphabetized, categorized, prioritized,* and *notarized.* I enthusiastically showed him my goals by timeline; 1-year goals, 3-year goals, etc. On the following pages, I showed him my goals by category; family, financial, health, and so on. On later pages, I showed how they were all prioritized by importance. After about two minutes of discussion, Dr. Qubein put one hand on my To-Do list and his other hand on my shoulder, looked me right in the eye over the top of his glasses and said, *"Doug, this is the best **To-Do** list I've ever seen."* This brought a big smile to my face and I remember thinking, *affirmation feels good*, but it didn't last long.

Before I could say a word, he said, *"Now, let me see your **To-Be** list."* Just as quickly as it came, the smile on my face was gone. I'm sure the new look on my face was something like the one you get in high school when the teacher says it's time to turn in your semester assignment, and you think to yourself, *"Oh no! That's due today!"* I didn't have a To-Be list, nor had I ever put any thought into one, per se, but I immediately knew I should have.

The confidence in my posture and voice were gone. I sheepishly said, *"I don't have a **To-Be** list."* Dr. Qubein removed his glasses, folded them, and while putting them in his pocket said, *"There's your nugget."* and he began to walk away. I said, *"Wait, wait, wait just a minute. You can't leave me hanging like that. Please explain."*

With a smile on his face, he walked back over and crystalized the message. He said, *"Doug, everybody has a **To-Do** list, a never-ending log of activities that day-after-day, from sun-up to sun-down, commands their time and attention, but only the best-of-the-best know who they are trying to **become** in life's journey as well. They have a **To-Be** list"*

Have you ever noticed that once you become aware of something, you begin to see it all around you? It's like when you buy a new car because it is so unique and then overnight it's like everyone started copying you and buying your exact car! Well, I began to see it everywhere. Everyone was busy, wishing they had more time in the day to get things done, but few knew to what end. Then I noticed the people I respected the most, the ones that were living the most complete lives filled with happiness, relationships, wealth, passion, and meaning, offset the chaos with a To-Be list of some kind.

The truth is we need both, because a To-Do list gives you transactional clarity and a To-Be list gives you transformational direction and purpose, but a To-Do list is about secular things that fade over time, like fame, fans, and fortunes, whereas a To-Be list is about spiritual things that are eternal, like friends, family and faith. Your To-Do list will bring you **success**, and your To-Be list will bring you **significance**. That phrase,

Success and Significance, has been a key guiding philosophy in my life for many years. It is my reminder to always seek a balance of both.

This philosophical shift changed my life. It set in motion the creation of my initial To-Be list.

I want to be:
1. **A Man of Faith** – Be an example of 'faith over fear' for my family and for others. My faith should be evident in all I do. Live a life of obedience and submission to God and his word.
2. **Honorable** – Be a man that brings honor to my family in all I do. Period.
3. **Energetic and Optimistic** – Always have the energy and optimism towards life as a person much younger than my actual years. In other words, when I'm 60, hold on to the life lessons that provide wisdom, but have the energy of a positive and optimistic 30-year-old.
4. **Passionately Grateful** – Develop a constant 'attitude of gratitude'. Even during difficult or challenging times, always find something to be grateful for and throughout life, give sincere thanks to anyone and everyone that helps me.
5. **A Lifelong Learner** – Be forever improving. Challenge my conditioned thoughts and beliefs. Read something new every day. Collect quotes from great thinkers and capture my thoughts in a journal for later reflection.
6. **Open to Change** – Be a person that is eager to embrace change. Remember, the past is a great place to visit, but it's a lousy place to live. For the timid, change is frightening; for the comfortable, change is threatening; but for the confident, change is always seen as opportunity.
7. **An Example of Love** – Be known for openly sharing and receiving love, the most important emotion of all. In the end, nothing else really matters except relationships. Be kind, compassionate, forgiving, and open my heart to others, especially my wife and children. Make sure they feel deep and unconditional love throughout their lives.

Here's how having a To-Be list manifested itself in my life.

Before I began to apply this life changing principle, I thought success was something I needed to pursue with tireless effort and resolve. I would set goals and with pig-headed discipline do my best to chase them down into submission. Such an approach is intense, stressful, and exhausting.

But then I realized that in nature, whatever you pursue eludes you. It's like chasing butterflies or herding cats. This was a really big ah-ha for me, and it completely changed my approach. Over time I learned that success wasn't something I needed to pursue, it was something I needed to attract, by the person I *become*. I still have to-do lists, primarily so I use my time wisely, but my main focus has shifted from what I need to pursue to who I need to become.

The application of my To-Be list wasn't completely positive, however. There is a drawback to having a To-Be list if you don't use it properly, and I learned it the hard way. Shortly after I created my To-Be list, I couldn't wait to share it with my family. After hearing the list, my son Clay, who was 5 years old at the time asked about my desire to be honorable? He asked, *"Dad, what does it mean to bring honor to the family?"* I did my best to explain that everything we do reflects on every member of our family and that I wanted my behavior to always uplift our name in the community, and to always make my family proud.

Three days later I was driving down the freeway with my family on our way to dinner when a sports car came out of nowhere and passed me at a very high rate of speed. He had to be going at least 100 mph and he barely missed the front of my vehicle as he changed into my lane. I was in the middle of three lanes and another car was slightly ahead of me in the left lane. How that sports car fit in that small gap still escapes me, especially at that speed. The margin for error was razor thin and his dangerous actions infuriated me. If he had clipped the front of our vehicle at that speed, I would have most likely lost control of the car, and God only knows what could have happened.

The vision in my mind of my vehicle swirling out of control and my family possibly being hurt activated the warrior instinct in me that wants to protect my family at all cost, so I lost it. I floored the gas pedal, the engine roared and I began screaming at the driver of the sports car. I made a few aggressive gestures with my fist and repeatedly motioned for him to pull over as I tried to catch him. This went on for about 30 seconds as I weaved in and around cars trying to catch him, but there was no way. It wasn't long before he was completely out of sight. At that point, I let my foot off the gas pedal, returned to a normal rate of speed, and began to regain my composure. I was still breathing heavy when Clay, who was sitting in the farthest seat in the back yelled out, *"Dad, is that bringing honor to the family?"*

Without saying a word, my head and eyes slowly turned toward my wife, knowing exactly what was going to happen next. With her arms crossed she turned her face towards mine, tilted her head and raised her eyebrows inquisitively as if to say, *"Yes Doug, does it? H-m-m-m."*

I looked back at the road in front of me with a blank stare on my face and although I just wanted to ignore my son or tell him to be quiet, my reply was simply, *"No son. That does not bring honor to the family, and I shouldn't have behaved that way."* Then through gritted teeth I added, *"Thanks for bringing it to my attention."* To this day my wife and I both laugh about this shining moment in my past, when my 5-year old son was my teacher. Thankfully, my wife turned a negative into a positive that evening when she told me how proud she was of me and that through humility, I showed great strength.

Here's my point. If used incorrectly, a To-Be list can leave you feeling shame or guilt, which are two of the most destructive words in the English language. They serve no one and they are always about the past, never the future. You must remember it is a "To-Be" list, not an "Already Doing" list, which means you still have work to do.

Having your own To-Be list will not prevent you from making mistakes. It won't make you perfect overnight, but it will help you correct your course much quicker when you veer off track. The goal is progress not perfection. Don't let your To-Be list be an albatross around your neck. Use it to help you communicate your desires to yourself and others so you'll correct your actions when you fall short.

I think you'll find, like I have, that when you say or do something that is out of alignment with your To-Be list, it will feel like a punch in the gut, which is a good thing because it will serve as a call to action. When you get that feeling all you have to do is immediately walk back to that person and say, *"I'm sorry. That does not reflect the kind of person I am or want to be. Can I have a do-over?"* You will be amazed at how energizing this is. Everyone can relate to falling short so you will not only be forgiven, you will be admired for being a person that has a clearly defined To-Be list, and for having the courage to admit your mistakes.

About Doug

Doug Hanson is a renaissance man in the world of motivation and business peak performance. His breadth of skills and services position him as a strategic resource for his corporate clients. He's been called the *Master of Motivation* and the *Ambassador of Ambition*, but he aspires to be a Transformation Coach, because he prefers the lasting nature of transformation. He teaches his clients that for motivation to last it must come from intrinsic drivers, not extrinsic perks or speeches. That everything we do and every decision we make is influenced by our current emotions and patterns of thought. Motivation derived from words or treasure is quick to fade, but an improvement in the quality of one's thinking and their ability to maximize their emotional state will change their life forever.

Doug is a highly sought-after speaker with a hilarious and engaging style that captivates his audiences. He has done presentations around the world with clients in the U.S., Canada, Mexico, Singapore, China, India, and many countries across Europe. On several occasions Doug has addressed audiences from more than 40 countries in a single event. In addition to his vast list of Fortune 500 clients, Doug was a featured facilitator and speaker at Tony Robbins' famous *Life Mastery University* in Hawaii for seven consecutive years, and was sought out by the NFL to energize the 10,000 volunteers involved in Super Bowl XXXVIII at the pre-game rally held in Houston's Reliant Stadium two weeks prior to the big game.

In addition to keynotes, half-day, and full-day seminars, Doug helps business leaders create a high-performance culture through a combination of services including assessments, teambuilding initiatives, leadership training, skills workshops, and his one-of-a-kind online employee engagement platform called MetaMorePhosis®. His employee engagement system is easy to initiate and Is based on his proven results around what he calls the four pillars of performance: *Skills, Mindset, Energy, and Connection.*

One thing that separates Doug from other premier speakers and consultants is that he does not force the same canned material across all clients and projects. Doug researches and tirelessly prepares for each engagement to insure his presentations and trainings align with each client's unique business objectives and event themes.

You can connect with Doug at any of the following websites:

- www.DougHanson.com
- www.MetaMorePhosis.com
- www.PlayFullOutOnline.com
- www.Twitter.com/MoreFromDoug
- www.Facebook.com/DougHansonSpeaker
- www.Linkedin.com/in/DougHanson281